RIDING FREE

by

Shuna Mardon

VOLTURNA PRESS

Copyright © 1985   Mrs. Shuna Mardon

ISBN   0 85606 141 7

Published by Volturna Press,   Hythe, Kent, U.K.

First published 1985

Typeset in 12 on 13pt Pyramid
by David J. Ellis
West Chiltington, West Sussex

Printed and bound in Great Britain by
Billing and Sons Limited
Worcester

CONTENTS

ILLUSTRATIONS

ACKNOWLEDGEMENTS FOR PHOTOGRAPHS

Frontispiece Leslie Lane, Burgess Hill, Sussex.
Plate 2 Marston Photographics.
Plate 3 Mark Fiennes Studios, Dorset.
Plate 6 A. M. Smith, Aberdeen.
Plate 7 Leslie Lane, Burgess Hill, Sussex.

FOREWORD

IN THIS book Shuna Mardon shows that she has a tremendous
wealth of experience behind her, of working with all different
kinds of animals. From breeding rabbits, showing donkeys,
training dogs, and now working with the horses she loves. She
has evented, shown side-saddle and won driving, to name but
a few of her successes. Strathdon and Shuna drew a lot of
attention working without a bridle, but this horse was a
challenge others would not have taken on. Shuna may have
had to use some unconventional methods to train her, but
what was finally achieved was a tremendous reward for
dedication and patience on the rider's part. Since then,
several other horses have been broken and brought on in the
same way, showing that this is no gimmick.

Shuna herself comes from a strong family background —
and it's just as well, considering all that she does in her day
to day routine. As well as specialising in her riding, she runs a
very successful stud and teaching yard, topped with helping
on the farm and bringing up a family. Most of us would
weaken!

Shuna's American Quarter Horse stud is producing an
extremely versatile animal. Her success in Western riding,
both at home and internationally, speaks for itself. Her
stallion, Waccabuc, is a medium dressage horse, and competes
show-jumping and cross-country. Her youngstock are now
being placed and winning in conventional hunter youngstock
classes. All of this proves to me that we will see even more of
Shuna and her Quarter Horses in all aspects of equestrianism

in the future in this country. A credit to her life-long hard
work and dedication.

Ian D. Stark

INTRODUCTION

ALL my life, as far back as I can remember, I have loved animals, especially horses. From the age of eleven I knew my ambition was to own and run a stud farm. Throughout my school days my parents and teachers tried to persuade me to change my mind, but I knew it was the only life for me. My otherwise patient mother could never see why anyone should want to breed horses, which when young are clumsy and stupid; that her own daughter should want to do so was startling. Nevertheless, she has always completely backed my sister and me in any venture we tried. It is certainly due to her long-suffering support that we both owe a great deal of our success in our rather unusual and exciting lives.

When at boarding school I often had the opportunity to visit the Police Dog Training Centre at Imber Court, just outside London. I was so impressed with the wonderful partnership which is built up between a police dog and his handler that I believed horses could be worked in the same way. However, most people contended that, owing to their size and assumed lack of brains, they could never be trusted to work without a strong form of direct control. I did not agree with this theory but at the same time I did not know how to start training a horse in any other way.

CHAPTER ONE

FOR many years after leaving school I concentrated my attention on building up a stud farm from a very small beginning, and almost forgot my theories on working horses without a bridle.

Then, in the summer of 1966, I came in contact with the horse which was, one day, to prove all my theories to be possible. I had travelled to the south of Scotland to compete in an important dressage competition run at a place called Dryden, near Selkirk. The MacAulays, who were organising the competition, had a wonderful old event mare, Flick, who was still breeding at the age of twenty-three. That year she had produced a very pretty, bright chestnut filly with pure white mane and tail. She was by the Arab stallion Horaya but, although very attractive, was not my type of animal, as I preferred the big, strong, hunter type of horse.

Over the next three years I saw the filly quite frequently but did not take much notice of her. During this time, Jean MacAulay lost three young horses with the dread grass sickness disease, including the chestnut filly's full brother. All this family of horses have exceedingly high-couraged temperaments, and in the wrong hands they can be very difficult and even dangerous. However, Jean decided she must sell the chestnut filly in case she also fell victim to the disease, which seems to affect young horses more than older ones. Knowing that I knew and understood this family, as I already owned a brood mare out of old Flick, and that I trained horses by patience rather than force, she tried to persuade me to buy the filly. I demurred because she was not my type of horse, but Jean offered her on very reasonable terms and included a guarantee to buy her back if I found I could not get on with her highly-strung temperament.

Against my better judgement I bought her — and began to regret my decision before I even got her home. At this stage she had been well handled, but unbroken, and therefore had never been in a horse-box, so we had to load her via a ramp and a sheep-pen, giving her no escape route. During the entire six-hour journey she never stopped kicking and pawing the box, working herself into such a state of sweat that the steam was coming out of the windows. On arrival home I turned her out into a large field, and by next morning she seemed quite settled, but when I brought her into a loose box to begin to get acquainted, she bolted out again. This she did three times — first she broke the bolt, then the hinges, and finally, when the fittings held, she crashed right through the door. In desperation I ran two strong iron bars the full length of the front of the box, and when she failed to get through them she attacked the wall between her stall and the one next to it with her heels. Having made a gaping hole about four feet wide, through which she could see the horse next door, she finally settled down.

By this time I considered the animal to be almost mad — but it would therefore be a challenge to try to break her. In the next few days I spent a great deal of time just working round the filly, which I had decided to name Strathdon, or Don for short. I handled and brushed her whilst talking to her all the time, to build up her confidence in me. Although extremely jumpy, she was certainly intelligent, and by the end of four days I could handle her all over, including crawling under her tummy without any sign of apprehension on her part. I consider the time spent really getting to know your horse and gaining his trust very important for all future training. No matter what type of work I am doing with my horses, I always try to gain their willing co-operation rather than to dominate them. I am sure this creates a much closer relationship between the horse and rider, which is invaluable when one is faced with problems later on in training or working the horse.

What was clearly shown in her reaction to being confined in a stable was that when faced with a new situation which either worried or frustrated her, Don would fight it rather than give in. The first priority was to gentle her and teach her riding manners without dominating her, which was unlike my usual methods. Normally, I like to have a few arguments with a young horse in the early stages so that I can discipline him and teach him obedience without having to be rough.

Any type of force used on Don would create an all-out battle, which I was not certain I could win. Therefore, for a couple of days after getting to know her in the stable, I led her about the farm, teaching her my words of command, and being firm yet never rough. On the third day I put the lungeing cavesson on and started teaching her to work in circles round me. This was October in her third year of age, and she was a very fat, hairy baby, so I tried to keep the work very slow. However, once she got the idea of going round in a circle she had other ideas of her own. I do not know whether she was afraid of the long lunge line or of the whip, which I never had to use, or if she just disliked the monotony of being confined to a small circle. She suddenly set off at a full gallop and, every time I tried to slow her by bringing her towards me, she plunged madly in the air and fought the line with all her strength. To avoid a real battle on the first day of training, I decided to let her gallop herself into the ground till she decided to stop of her own accord. But I got increasingly worried that she might kill herself before giving in, for she galloped without stopping for twenty-five minutes. I had never known a horse do this before, and when she finally came to a halt she was lathered in sweat, with water running off her tummy and legs. I just hoped she had learnt that nothing had hurt her and that she would accept the exercise more easily the next day. I made a great fuss of her and spent the next hour walking her dry but always leading her close up to her head to prevent a repeat performance.

For the next three days she repeated the mad galloping, but luckily for a shorter spell each time, and when she came to a halt I just quietly asked her to "walk on". By the end of the fourth lesson, after two sessions of galloping, she at last relaxed and moved round me at a walk. This was a major step forward in our relationship and she had begun to trust me.

I had to trace-clip her before she lost too much condition. The feel and noise of a clipper for the first time terrifies most horses, but Don accepted it, showing little or no fear.

After this stage her basic training went off smoothly, with all the work being done by me, although the girls did handle her at times in the stable. Once she had accepted the idea of training, she was quick to learn and, apart from bucking the first time she wore a saddle, she gave little more trouble. By the time I came to back her she had such confidence in anything I did with her that she did not seem to notice the fact that I was on top of her. She stood quietly as I jumped half on and off again, then threw my leg right over her and moved about on her back, all the time talking to her. She did not try to buck, and within a very few days she was going for short rides, with the reins attached to the lungeing cavesson. It was better not to interfere with her mouth at this stage.

Next, we hit our problem. Don obviously enjoyed going out for rides with the other horses and seeing new country, but she always wanted to be in the lead at whatever pace, and would resist any restrictions on her. She did this by fighting the reins, whether they were on the cavesson or the bit, throwing her head and running away. As I hoped to do dressage with her eventually, I was afraid she might ruin her mouth in this fighting, and I knew I had to find some other way of riding her.

CHAPTER TWO

BELIEVING it possible to develop such a close relationship between a horse and his rider that the animal will do anything asked of him without the use of force, I also considered that a horse could be ridden in all types of work without the use of a bridle, bit or other contraption of control.

However, I did not know where to start, until a chance meeting in 1969, when my husband and I were on holiday in Bermuda. There we came upon an American horseman by the name of John O'Neill.

John O'Neill had lived with horses all his life, had worked as a cowboy, raced stock horses, worked and ridden in rodeos and was now in Show business. In the years to come we built up a friendship and I was to learn a great deal of horsemanship from him. When my husband Philip and I first went to stay with his family in New York State, I discovered an interesting thing: John rode his horses without a bridle.

Philip and Mrs O'Neill were not interested in horses, so soon after our arrival John took me out to see his part Quarter Horse mare, Lady Q. She was a lovely deep sorrel, with the most intelligent expression. John proceeded to ride her for half an hour under a Western saddle with no bridle, only a light strap round her neck. Although working Western, he was performing all types of schooling movements up to medium dressage standard, and the thing that impressed me most was the complete at-oneness between horse and rider. Lady Q was so obviously listening for his next command, without any anticipating, and with an obvious desire to please her rider.

Immediately I realised that this was the type of horsemanship I had been looking for over the past fifteen years. During the next ten days I spent many hours studying John's methods of gaining confidence and trust. When he starts riding a young horse, he teaches him the basic aids by using a very simple "Bosal" hackamore, which is a loose, rigid noseband made of plaited rawhide. When he feels the horse and he have gained mental communication he takes the bridle off and does not use it again for any future training.

With many new ideas on horsemanship, including a strong liking for the Western style of riding, I returned home to try them out on my fiery little mare. It was a challenge to me. If John could do it, being away from home so much on his Show business, then so could I. However, my plans had to wait for a few months, as at this time I was expecting our twin boys.

During the next two months I did not have much time for my horses but had a very good girl running the stud. Following John's ideas on building up a one-man relationship with one's horse, I did manage to spend a few hours every day working with Don.

When I had got my family into a manageable routine, I was once more back in the saddle. After a few months of close contact but very little riding, I found Don glad to be able to get out on the trails again. She accepted the control aids quite easily on the Bosal, which I had brought back from America, although she still disliked the bit. I worked Don round about our home ground for three months, building up a strong trust between us, always sure that anything I did, or asked her to do, would not hurt her. She was now in her four-year-old year, and I introduced her to very small jumps, both natural objects and painted poles, and she obviously loved jumping. I was also beginning to feel a close rapport with her which I had never quite felt with any other horse.

One day I felt she was now listening to my leg aids, and we definitely had a strong mental communication, which I think is essential in some degree in this type of training. I left the bridle at home and set out on our ride with a light strap round Don's neck. Working in the English style I had taught her entirely on leg aids, using the neck strap only to prepare her for a new command. When working Western one can use the neck strap to assist in steering, but this is useless when jumping.

On the first day I rode Don about three miles along bridle trails at all paces, then took her into my schooling field and did twenty minutes in basic schooling exercises. Never in the whole ride did I get the feeling that she was not going to do what I asked of her.

Our mutual confidence in each other grew steadily over the next few months. After the first day I never put the bridle on again, not even in strange situations or to teach new movements. From then on Don did all her learning bridle-less until much later when I started to retrain her for dressage, when use of a bridle is a necessary rule in competing. As I was careful to make sure she understood what was wanted of her before presenting new problems, by the end of a year from starting this work she understood my aids and I could introduce new situations exactly as if I were using a bridle, and often with better results. This was especially true where jumping was concerned; a horse jumping with its head completely free can use itself so much better than one who relies on the bit contact for balance and control. I was now jumping Don frequently, and in all her training she never once ran out at a fence, which can seldom be said of a horse even working under ordinary conditions. She would tackle all types of obstacle, including water, with the same confidence that what I wanted of her could be done. These few months of building up this close relationship probably gave me the greatest pleasure I have ever had in horsemanship. The one problem of a close relationship with an animal is the emotional involvement.

Plate 1. Strathdon competing in an endurance ride, where she won a silver award, in the 1973 Golden Horseshoe 75-mile ride. See Chapter 14.

CHAPTER THREE

JOHN first discovered his ability to work a horse without a bridle by chance, soon after he had bought a grade Quarter Horse called Stepper.

This was just after he had started a very successful career in Show business, and he had gone to a stable to buy a good Quarter Horse. He rode one of their rent horses which was very unpopular with most people. This was Stepper, a Quarter type buckskin which had probably had very rough handling as a youngster and did not like humans. Unless the rider was very strong he could not cope with him nor make him go where wanted; thus he was not much use in a rent string. John, however, found something special in him. When he tried to buy Stepper, the owner was horrified and said he had much better horses to offer. Eventually, as the stable was glad to get rid of the horse, John was able to buy him for $125. He spent the next few months getting to know the independent character of the horse and building up trust. Although Stepper was an eight-year-old he had never known real love and respect from man.

Stepper resented all kinds of force, but John soon established a relationship in which the horse co-operated willingly. While playing around with Stepper round his home, John found he was able to ride him easily with only a rope round his neck, or even nothing at all. He then proceeded to develop a few simple leg aids, and never again needed to use a bridle even when competing in fast mounted games or when crossing dangerous country on major cross-country rides.

During his early years in Show business, John had a great deal of spare time to spend with Stepper and they used to go on many big trail rides all over the country. These rides often lasted up to a week, covering more than two hundred miles of tough, exciting countryside. During overnight stops, all the horses were tied up to a picket line, but John never had to tie Stepper up. When they arrived at a camp site, John would slip off and Stepper would take himself down to the nearest watering place and then return to John, who would unsaddle him and give him his feed and hay along the picket line, and there Stepper would stay without being tied until John called him next morning.

Many of John's friends did not believe that any horse could be trusted this far, and used to challenge him to test Stepper's reliability. One day when there were over a hundred horses in camp, John, to prove his point, made bets with his friends that they could saddle up all the other horses in camp and ride out, and that Stepper would stay by the picket line alone as long as he knew that John was still in camp. Most of them thought he was mad, but took him on. John sat on some rocks about twenty-five yards from the picket, saying nothing, while the others saddled up and rode out together. Stepper watched them go, but remained standing quietly by the line. When the agreed time had passed, some of the riders returned and had to admit that John had won the bets, which totalled about $300.

When John was showing off, as he used to do in the early days, Stepper would always take care of him. Sometimes when negotiating very steep rocky slopes, other riders got very worried when their horses were tripping and losing their footing, but John used to turn round in the saddle and sit facing the tail, leaving Stepper to pick his way down the slope on his own.

This mutual trust saved Stepper's life on at least one occasion. John and a friend were cutting new trails in the mountains above Los Angeles, and were crossing a very steep slope covered in loose boulders and scree, when Stepper, who was in the lead, tried to stop at a washed-out gully. However,

John urged him forward, and within a few strides the loose stones began to give way under his feet. He tried desperately to scramble up onto firmer ground, but started sliding downhill into a steep, narrow gully, where John got knocked off against the rocky sides. Stepper ended up wedged between two sheer faces of rock rising about sixteen feet above him and about twenty-five feet of very steep gully behind him and a drop of a few hundred feet below. The gully was so narrow that John could not get down beside him, and there was no way they could pull him up with a rope because of the narrowness of the gully. So hopeless did the situation look that a friend suggested that the kindest thing to do would be to shoot him before he panicked and broke his back or neck. However, John was determined not to lose his faithful friend so easily and was able to climb down onto the rocks directly above the horse. By gently coaxing and talking to Stepper he was able to induce the horse to back himself slowly up the gully to solid ground and safety, his trust in his owner being stronger than the instinct to panic. Although badly bruised and shaking, he was not seriously injured, and maintained this close relationship with John for the rest of his life, even though the accident had been John's mistake.

For over ten years John and Stepper rode in parades and displays, a saddle being the only tack Stepper ever wore. Sometimes John would run away from Stepper and hide, but the horse would immediately find him, by scent if not by sight. Many people think horses are not capable of ''scenting'' out. When tales of Stepper's behaviour were being discussed with a group of knowledgeable horsemen, they wouldn't believe them, but when they saw with their own eyes they said the horse was loco and the man mad.

On the only time when someone else tried to ride Stepper without a bridle, the horse panicked and bolted wildly for nearly a mile, although the man was an experienced rider. This was due to a lack of that communication between horse and rider which is the basis of my own experiences.

Plate 2.
*Miss Bay Charger, who also worked for me without
a bridle after I bought her from John O'Neill.
See Chapter 23.*

CHAPTER FOUR

UP TO this stage of the work I had persevered with this method of training purely for my own satisfaction and to prove the possibility of a theory I had held for many years. But I had no idea where it would lead us in the future. I knew from John O'Neill's experience that most conventional horsemen would laugh and claim it impossible to be in complete control without a bridle, or say it was being done as a gimmick to show off. For these reasons, and the fact that most of my friends thought I was mad, I kept quiet, while enjoying each new step in my mare's schooling and in her obvious pleasure in working free. Because her head was completely free, her jumping style was more natural than that of any other young horse I had worked. In some photographs her nose is actually seen to be lower than her forefeet while over the fence, thus creating a tremendous bascule and allowing greater use of her back.

One day, while teaching a local Riding Club class, I was confronted by two young ladies mounted on nice, big four-year-olds. They were both wearing pelham bits, standing martingales, and one also had a dropped noseband. When I expressed my horror at such severe tack on young horses, I was told they were both unstoppable. For their age they were well schooled and great jumpers, I was told, and they had competed frequently, but without this severe tack they both tended to bolt wildly, especially when being asked to jump. When I suggested that neither horse had been properly schooled or taught basic manners and school movements, and that I suspected the poor animals simply did not understand what was required of them, the riders laughed. I stated that if a horse was properly broken and schooled he could easily be ridden in any type of bit, or no bit at all. This statement had no effect, and in self-defence I said I would demonstrate it at the next rally, to prove my point.

I had now committed myself to putting my theories to the test in public, and several times before the day I wished I had kept my mouth shut. These rallies usually bring out about twenty-five people, but on this day seventy-two turned up. Perhaps the word had got around that something unusual might happen, and I felt that many of my audience thought I was going to make a fool of myself. I had laid out a small arena with barrels, a small obedience test, and four small jumps, all on the top of a hill, as it was October and this was the only area clear of mud. The day was cold and clear, with a wind. Don was now a well-developed four-year-old, clipped out, and exceedingly full of herself.

By this time I had taught Don to work under Western as well as English tack, and I had planned to show the youngsters some Western movements, followed by basic dressage work and then jumping. At first Don was very excited by all the people, but I jogged her round while I explained what her basic schooling had been and demonstrated the very simple leg aids which I used to guide and control her. At this stage I was working with a light strap round her neck, which I used to draw her attention to me and warn her that I was about to give her a command by leg aids. The leg aids were based on usual dressage aids, as I intended to do dressage with her, using a bridle, in the future. My aids were simply pressure from both legs on the girth, which meant move forward or increase speed, and both legs further back, combined with a fairly strong seat, meant slow down, halt, or rein back if already halted. My turning aids were inside leg on the girth, outside leg back, and the quicker I wished to turn, the stronger I applied the aids. By the end of Don's training, I could achieve a fast halt from a good gallop, and a tight 360° turn from all paces.

Having settled my horse and got my audience thinking, I started off my display by demonstrating the use of the aids in simple movements. I then went on to the early stages of lateral work, showing that if a horse is correctly bent round the rider's inside leg, the even curve will be maintained throughout her body, from head to tail. Having changed into an English saddle, I finished off with a simple obedience test, including work over poles, bending round obstacles, and reining back through a "Z" pattern of poles. This was followed by four jumps, including a combination which I repeated. But on the second time I halted in the centre, turned off and then jumped the whole thing again, to prove that my horse was neither running away, nor anticipating nor fighting, but being exceedingly obedient.

The kids were delighted, and their elders, I think, surprised rather than impressed, but they all agreed they had a lot to take away and think about. Unknown to me, one of the fathers had been taking photographs, and a month later one of the horsey magazines printed a full page of Don working without a bridle, and that was the end of my keeping this work private.

Now that I no longer had a reason to keep this work to myself, I began to think along lines of entering Don for competitions. By the time she was a rising five-year-old, I knew that for all her lack of size she was tough, exceedingly intelligent and had ability to jump. I am not very competitive minded and would never risk killing my horse to win, but I like to use competitions to prove to myself that I am working along the right lines and succeeding in my training.

For the usual showing and dressage classes, it is obligatory to wear a bridle and bit, so I started to remouth Don as I would a youngster. I rode Don in a Bosal, with a bit hanging in her mouth and got her used to the rein aids again before transferring the reins to the bit. I also had to teach her to work in a more collected manner: although she was always very well balanced and correctly bent, I had not tried to achieve true collection. But I decided never to jump her in a bridle with a bit, as it would be almost impossible to allow her the freedom of head and neck which she had been used to, while trying to steady her in a bridle on the approach to a fence. At this time there was no restriction on what type of bridle had to be worn in the jumping phase of horse trials or show jumping events.

Within a few weeks Don had accepted the new routine for school work, but she got very cross if I did not then remove the bridle before going out for hacking and jumping work. At this stage I noticed something which interested me in the mental side of a horse's character. Although Don accepted a bit and obeyed my rein aids almost perfectly, there was very much less mental communication between us than when she was working bridleless. I had also started to ride Don side-saddle as I consider straight showing a very good way to introduce a young horse to appearing in public, and Don did not fit into any of the usual classes. By riding her side-saddle she appeared as a lady's hunter, and so her lack of size did not matter so much.

All through her training, Don had been a "one-man" horse to me, and very much disliked being ridden by anyone else. Thus, for her first appearance in public I chose the local Riding Club's Summer Show, where she would not have to be ridden by the judges. She went very well side-saddle, to win the small hunter class, and came Reserve Champion overall. She was much admired and obviously enjoyed the attention; being able to show off is a great help when showing a horse. At this same Show I entered her in the Novice Jumping, working bridleless, much to the surprise of the audience, this being the first time she had appeared away from home. Don was quite unworried by her new surroundings and gave me two clear rounds, although unplaced as I did not want to hurry her.

I was, of course, delighted with this event and now took the plunge and entered Don in the Ridden Arab and Small Hunter classes at the Royal Highland Show. Before this big event I had one combined training event where she did a fair dressage test and another clear round jumping bridleless, to be in the placings.

On the first day of the big Show, I was showing young stock in the inhand classes, and had little time to work Don in before the Small Hunter class. As a result Don was very full of herself and excited by the huge arena. She did not show herself well against a very strong entry, not to mention bucking when the judge rode her, but by the next day and the Arab classes, she had settled down and showed beautifully, including going well for a nice lady judge. At the end of this class she finished third out of twenty-three entries, and I was delighted.

CHAPTER FIVE

OUR next expedition was to the annual Dressage event at Dryden, Selkirkshire, which was Don's birthplace. Jean Mac-Aulay had followed Don's career with great interest, having ridden members of the same family for many years, and known them all to be sensitive and of high courage. Being an experienced dressage rider, she realised the rapport necessary between horse and rider, but she was rather sceptical about how far one could go in open competition while riding the horse without a bridle.

Jean's neighbourhood had known Don's family for three generations and followed their various successes, so Jean asked me if I would give their local Riding Club an informal display of bridleless riding, the evening before the event. By this time I had Don's ground work fairly well polished and we were to work in the indoor school, this being the best place to seat the audience. Most of these people had never seen a Western saddle except on cowboy films, and I rode Don in one. I started by showing them how to fit the saddle, pointing out how it varied from an English one and what all the various parts of a Western Roping Saddle are used for. Then I mounted up and ran through a few basic schooling movements, which are almost the same in English or Western riding. I finished the flat work with some on two tracks, including shoulder-in and half-pass as for dressage, and then a fast canter into a fast halt and rein back, as used in Western schooling. This was followed by exercises over four small jumps and after these it was all over. My audience appeared

impressed but without great enthusiasm, and asked a few
questions.

Next morning was fine and sunny and the dressage started
early, with four judges working simultaneously in four
different rings, owing to the huge entry. I had Don down in
the dressage area by 10 a.m., getting her settled and worked
in for her first test at 10.30. The ground was very hard and
causing trouble with some of the big horses slipping, but I
had put studs in Don's shoes and she had no problems, doing
a very good test for the preliminary class. Within ten minutes
we were on in the Novice ring and she did another good test,
but not quite as smooth as her first one. This second test is
more advanced than the preliminary, the movements coming
more quickly after each other. There were one and a half
hours to spare before the Elementary test, which is even
more advanced, but I felt that Don was ready to have a go at
it. In the meantime I put Don back in the stable to rest while
I rode a Novice test on Fingal, which also went well, but he
was a much more experienced horse, though getting a bit
stiff in his back. By the time I was ready for the Elementary
test, the early dressage scores were on the board, and I was
very pleased to find that Don was lying second and third in
her respective tests, out of thirty entries in each class.
However, these two tests were part of a combined competition,
which meant that any faults incurred in the jumping phase
would be taken into account in deciding the winner.

The Elementary test was pure dressage and I tacked Don
up and gave her ten minutes to work-in. The horse-flies were
causing the horses to throw their heads and swish their tails,
in spite of their riders having used anti-fly spray. Remembering
an old hint I had once heard from a retired horseman, I went
back to where my horsebox was parked, got a piece of rag
and soaked it in diesel oil. One must be careful not to get the
oil onto the horse's skin. Don's mane was plaited but I dabbed
a little onto the top of a few plaits near her head and wiped
her tail with the rag, which was enough to make the whole
horse smell of diesel, which the flies hate. After this treatment
she did another smooth test, but lacked lengthening in the

extended trot work, although her counter-canter was "super". Some of the more advanced horses were very unsteady in this test and Don's smoothness and accuracy were enough to bring her up to third place in this class. I was very satisfied with the result.

Quickly after the Elementary dressage came the Riding Club Teams event, where teams of three riders from each Club compete on much the same lines as in a pairs class. They do an individual display, which is judged on their dressing and smoothness at all paces, then they are lined up and inspected for cleanliness and neatness and similarity of turnout. I was riding for the North East Riding Club from Aberdeenshire, and we had two of my horses and one other all turned out in Western gear. This certainly surprised the judge, but he accepted us and we did our display. We lost several points on similarity because there are so few Western saddles in this country and none of them are quite the same. We finished in fourth place.

Then another quick change into double bridle and show saddle for the small Working Hunter class. This class started off with a cross-country course including jumping up and down hill and over water. I had to wear a bridle to comply with the rules, but rode Don on as loose a rein as possible, and she gave me a clear round, obviously enjoying the change from boring dressage. The rest of the class is judged as for an ordinary show hunter class, and was very drawn out owing to the large number of entries. In the end Don was placed fifth, and we made a quick exit to get ready for the other jumping events.

For the jumping section of the combined training events there was no rule stating that I had to wear a bridle, so Don came cantering into the ring obviously delighted to be free. The effect on the audience was electric. Although some of them had seen my display the evening before, I think that none believed I would appear out in the open, in a competition, without a bridle. Don was, however, quite unimpressed by their astonishment and proceeded to do a lovely, flowing clear round which included an awkward combination fence.

The horse which led in the dressage had two fences down and this gave Don a clear win in the Preliminary class, to the applause from her surprised audience. In the next class, where the jumps are higher, she again did a good round, with one pole off the stile, which brought her into third place in this class. As may be imagined, we spent the remainder of the day the centre of attraction. Jean was thrilled; she had had much fun in the past competing on Don's mother and she could see similarity in this unusual daughter.

Our next event was the Scottish Horse Show, held at the Royal Highland Showground near Edinburgh, at the end of August each year. It is an important Show, the finals of the qualifying events held throughout the year being held here. Because of this, the jumping classes were too advanced for Don at this stage, but there is a Handy Horse class judged partly on obedience, partly on jumping and partly on conformation. There are no restrictions on the type of bridle to be worn and I rode bridleless. While I was working-in outside the main arena, one of the stewards, who is also a well-known Master of Foxhounds, asked me if I intended actually competing without a bridle. When I said I did, he seemed pleased, and, unknown to me, he carefully arranged for me to enter the ring first. Then he stopped all the other competitors at the entrance and announced that all entrants in this class were to ride "bridleless". When they laughed incredulously he simply pointed to me with a serious expression on his face. The resulting chaos and queries from worried competitors in the collecting ring must have been entertaining. After about five minutes of this, the steward relieved them from their suspense and allowed them to enter normally.

Don did all that was asked of her and gained top marks on obedience, but lost points on type and conformation, ending up fourth out of a very big class. At the end the judge came up and admired the beauty of the natural way my horse performed while still showing perfect control. This was probably the highest compliment we were paid that year, and he was a very well-known hunter judge.

To finish off the season I rode Don in a couple of Riding Club one-day events, where she went well. In the first one she gave me a good test and went clear both cross-country and show jumping, working bridleless; but I did not hurry her so was unplaced. The second one was at Dryden, where George MacAulay had built a cross-country course with a pen or "V" fence in the middle, which was causing a great deal of concern amongst the competitors as they walked the course. At these events I liked to keep Don away from the main crowd, partly to keep her settled, and partly to avoid all the questions as to "How and Why" I had decided to ride without a bridle. As a result, not many people noticed that I had taken off the bridle after the dressage, where she had done a good test. The few people who were working near me all had the same question: "How are you going to tackle the 'V' fence?" My answer was then, and still is, that I did not have any definite plan. Unknown to me, Jean, who had ridden earlier in the class, threw her horse at her daughter, saying she must see how Don coped with this bogey fence which was causing such trouble.

I learnt more about mental communication on that course. Don and I set off at a good steady pace and she gave me a wonderful feeling; she neither rushed her fences nor had to be pushed into them. I could feel her steady herself once she realised I wanted her to jump a certain obstacle or part of a wall, then just lengthen her stride on the approach as I rode for the fence. She was jumping freely and easily and the going was good, so we both enjoyed the experience. The main problem with the "V" fence was that one approached it along a track which went straight on, while the course turned sharp left after jumping the first element into the "V", and, exactly one stride away, one should jump out over the second side of the "V". There was, however, nothing to stop the horse carrying straight on along the track and so running round the side of the second part of the jump. I was not aware of doing anything different as we approached this fence, but when we jumped the first element I indicated to Don, both mentally and with my leg aids, that I wished to turn left. The result was that she did a smooth turn in mid air, landed, took one stride and jumped easily out over the second part.

Jean told me later that Don had jumped it better than any other horse that day, because there had been no interference with her balance and freedom, as would have been the case with a bridle. At the end of the cross-country phase, I was in the lead, and these hunting people were impressed because I could do this bridleless riding right out in the open and going fast. Unfortunately, I was feeling so pleased with Don and myself that I did not work her in sufficiently for the jumping phase, and we had the rail off the top of the first fence, which dropped us down to third. However, even this stupid mistake could not dampen the pleasure I had on the cross-country ride, which I regarded as the toughest test to which I had so far put Don's trust.

This event brought our first season in public to an end, and the only other thing I did with Don in 1971 was to take her hunting with the Buccleuch Hounds. I rode her in a bosal, as I was not at all sure what her reactions would be and felt that in the excitement of hunting she possibly would not listen to my leg aids, and mental communication would be less as the excitement grew. She did get very excited and we had a wonderful fast day. At the end of it I decided that one day I would take up probably the greatest challenge—I would hunt Don without a bridle, but this would have to wait in the meantime.

CHAPTER SIX

UP UNTIL this stage I had been enjoying the immense pleasure one can get from a really close relationship with an animal, but I had never thought about the emotional consequences which can result from such an involvement. All through my life I have been very attached to, and possibly sentimental about, my animals. Now I was beginning to realise that the feelings I had for Don, and the response I got back from her, were something far deeper and quite different from anything I had experienced before. However, I had not even considered the opposite effects, of how easily and deeply one can be hurt if things go wrong with the animal one is involved with. This was brought out very suddenly in a rather sad visit I made to the O'Neills in Waccabuc, New York, in the autumn of 1971.

Now that it was public knowledge that a mad lady in Aberdeenshire was actually competing on a horse without a bridle, news and gossip spread fast, and I found myself being asked to go to give talks to various groups of people on my methods of training. In ten minutes I can tell someone the aids I use, but no one can teach a person how to develop a feeling with an animal. So I found it very difficult to keep people's interest for two hours, which is the usual time a guest speaker is expected to entertain the audience. As I had done this work purely for my own interest, I had taken only a few short pieces of film of Don's work, and now I desperately needed facts and film as proof of my theories.

By this time our boys were a year old, and I had not had

a real break since they were born. Philip, my husband, was
going off on a shooting safari to Africa, which was not the
kind of holiday I would enjoy; also, we did not both want to
be away from our family and the farm at the same time. So
by fitting in our absences I arranged to return to New York,
where I hoped to take a few hundred feet of film showing
John training his horses, partly working them conventionally
as for cattle work, and partly going through his work without
a bridle. This was to be useful to back up my talks and let me
elaborate on general Western training as well as bridleless
work. My plans, however, were not to work out as expected.

I travelled out with an American student who had been
working on my stud that summer, and spent the first few
days with her family in Clinton, near Utica, a most pleasant
part of north New York.

When I reached Waccabuc, John met me and said he had
bad news. Little Lady Q had got a nail in her foot that day.
Although he had removed the old rusty nail and treated the
wound, and given her an anti-tetanus injection, she was still
lame and he doubted if she would be able to do the work
for the film I had hoped to make. However, we had nearly
two weeks, and these puncture wounds can often heal
quickly once the cause has been removed; Lady was certainly
not very bothered about it that night.

Next morning the picture was quite different. I had gone
out to the barn first and found Lady lying flat out, breathing
fast and sweating. I tried to get her to move without success,
so I rushed back to the house to catch John before he went
off to the City. When he came out to the barn, talking to her,
Lady raised her head and whinnied, but made no attempt to
get up. Kneeling beside her, John examined her and made an
effort to raise her. He said he felt sure it was just pain, but he
could not understand why.

Obviously the situation was beyond his control, so he called
the vet, who arrived quickly and by using an X-ray machine
discovered that some of the nail had broken off inside the
foot. When he had nerve-blocked the leg above the fetlock,
Lady stood up and was much more at ease. When asked for

his opinion on treatment and possible recovery, the vet said he could not tell. The only hope was to operate under a local anaesthetic, and cut away the sole of the foot until he had found and removed all the pieces of metal. He had never had to do this before and did not know how far he would have to go to remove all the foreign bodies; he guessed she had a fifty-fifty chance of recovery.

It was a ghastly decision for John to make; he was out of work at the time and had a young family to support, and, whatever the final result, the operation and further treatment would cost a great deal of money. It would also mean a considerable amount of suffering for Lady, but John had bought her as a tiny foal and they had been together ever since. She was now seven and had always worked for him without a bridle, lived near the house without ever being fenced in, and become very close to John. The only other option was to shoot her.

John decided to go ahead with the operation. He held Lady's head to keep her quiet, and I helped the vet where necessary, in what turned out to be one of the bloodiest operations I had ever seen. He had to cut away all the sole and one side of the frog, right to the wall, and go into the foot until he came to the coffin bone, where he found the pieces of nail which had broken off against the bone. Having cleaned out this big wound, the vet packed the foot hard, so that Lady could put wieght on it without the now almost exposed bone being moved. He strapped the packing on with tight bandages because we did not know where we could get a poultice boot. The vet said he had never before had to cut away so much of the strong sole tissue, but, as the bone structure did not appear to be damaged, he still gave her a fifty-fifty chance. Whatever the final result, there was going to be a great deal of very careful nursing required in the first ten days or so to prevent the wound going septic. This would mean removing the dressings twice daily and soaking the foot in special solution to promote healing. If Lady put her foot to the ground while the packing was out she would be finished, for there would be no support for the bone until

the strong tissues grew again. She would also require a heavy
pain-killing injection twice a day and, even so, there would be
a considerable amount of pain, at least for the first few days.
Leaving us with these encouraging words, the vet said he
could do no more.

With the local anaesthetic still having effect, Lady was
quite happy and started tucking in to her hay, while we made
her a deep bed, for we felt sure she would spend the time
lying down – a horse finds it difficult to stand on three legs
when the injured one is a foreleg. By afternoon Lady was
feeling very sorry for herself and soon hobbled over to her
bed, being loose in the large barn, and lay down. As I helped
John put hay and water within her reach I felt as sorry for
him as for the horse; Lady obviously looked to him for help
and there was so little he could do for her. I also realised how
easily Strathdon and I could be in the same situation and for
the first time I understood the consequences of getting too
emotionally involved with an animal. During the next few
days I had plenty of time to think about it, but finally decided
that the pleasure gained from close association with an animal
is worth the risk of being hurt.

John now had to spend many hours dressing Lady's foot
and trying not to think about the expense. I was glad I was
there, for it took two of us to do the job – one holding the
leg to prevent her standing on it, the other doing the bathing
and dressing. John's wife did not know much about horses
and neither did any of his neighbours in that part of New
York State. The first few days were very worrying and John
was not certain that he had made the right decision. Lady
spent practically all the time lying down, but always seemed
pleased to see John. After the first day she ate and drank
everything that was put within her reach. By the fourth day
things were looking better; there was no sign of infection
setting up in the foot and when the packing was in Lady
tentatively tried to put it to the ground. By the afternoon
she had managed to move right through the barn. However,
this increased activity caused other problems; by hopping
on three legs she was putting a tremendous strain on the other

foreleg, and by the next day the tendons were badly filled, and so we had to keep tight support bandages on that other leg. Lady was now determined to get out, and by the end of the first week she was able to graze at the back of the house, putting some weight on the injured foot. By the middle of the second week I had to leave for home, but by this time the dressing operation was much more simple, as we no longer had a raw, open wound. Although Lady did eventually become sound, it took three years and a lot of disappointment for John.

While on my last trip to America I had been determined to buy a Western saddle, for it was difficult to find a good one in Britain. However, New York State was not a good place to find Western tack either, for most people in that area rode English fashion. I looked in quite a few saddle stores but they seemed only to have the cheaper ones which would not stand up to the work I required of them. At last I came to a new store, which had a Tex Tan Roping saddle as the "Saddle of the Month" offer, which means that the makers of the saddle supply one of their brands at a greatly reduced price for the first month the new shop is open, to encourage customers to come to the shop. John, who was with me, said it was a very good saddle and the best bargain I was likely to find, so I bought it.

I had to take the train eighty miles into New York City and then get a taxi to Kennedy Airport to catch my plane home. As John said "Good-bye" and helped me onto the train with my big suitcase, two cameras, a handbag and the saddle (which weighed forty-five pounds) he also said he was sure I would be cursing the saddle before I got it home. At the time I laughed, little knowing how soon his words would come true. When the train neared the City it had to go underground, and just before we reached Central Station there was a shuddering jolt and the train came to a halt.

At first I thought nothing of it; trains always seem to get held up in the middle of nowhere or in a tunnel. After we had sat there for over an hour, passengers got restless and I got worried that I would miss my flight. After another half hour one of the guards told us that the front half of the train had become derailed and we were going to have to walk along the tunnel for nearly a mile to the station.

With a forty-pound suitcase and the awkward, heavy saddle, this was no joke. But there seemed to be no alternative. It was indeed a struggle! The space between the train and the wall of the tunnel was four feet wide, and the saddle alone was nearly three feet across. But eventually I reached the station — and to my horror found it was rush hour. I had an hour in which to get to the airport. New York in rush hour has to be seen to be believed; the pavements are a seething mass of people and the streets are jammed solid with six lanes of traffic almost always at a standstill. I kept knocking into people with the saddle, and finding a taxi seemed remote. Then a teenage girl unexpectedly came out of the crowd and asked me where I came from. When I told her Scotland, she looked very surprised and said she thought I must have come from The West because of the saddle. I briefly told her my situation and she offered to get me a taxi, and disappeared. I did not expect to see her again, but in about five minutes she drew up in a taxi and bundled me and all my luggage inside. I scribbled my address on a match box and handed it to the girl, but I doubt if I will ever see her again. I certainly owe her my heartfelt thanks for the fact that I just caught the plane at the last moment.

I intended taking the saddle on the plane as hand luggage and was carrying it unwrapped. I might have got away with this on one of the Western inter-state lines, but this particular line was certainly not going to allow it. I did not want it to go baggage, unwrapped, because of the risk of damage, and I found myself on the floor of the busy passenger terminal with yards of string and brown paper, to the amusement of fellow travellers. I got aboard the aircraft complete with all my belongings, exhausted and with a strained arm muscle.

The saddle has given me great service over seven years and thousands of miles of riding, and I hope it will last for many years to come. It was well worth all the trouble of getting it to Britain.

CHAPTER SEVEN

DURING the many hours spent helping John with Lady, I had had a great deal of time to discuss various ways of schooling horses, and had developed an interest in the American Quarter Horse, which was the type of horse with which John had usually worked, and in the Western way of riding developed over the years by the cowboys. These men spent most of their lives in the saddle, doing a job of work at the same time. They had devised an exceedingly comfortable saddle and expected their horses to get on with the job in hand without always having to rely on the rider's aids.

There are many different approaches to Western riding. Some cowboys do the job mainly because they love the life and their horses, and horse and rider enjoy working together. Others ride because they have to, to do their job, and make use of the horse as though it were a machine. Although often very good horsemen they want quick results, and tend to use force in the form of severe bits and spurs, reinforced by the use of a tight martingale, known as a tie-down. Some will even go as far as using barbed wire to teach a horse to become light to the neck rein or the hackamore.

When I came home I spent much time through the winter months teaching Don to be a good Western mount in the manner of the dedicated cowboys. Owing to her natural sensitivity it was easy to teach her to neck-rein, and she already knew how to do a fast stop and reasonably quick turns, although the Arab type of horse finds it hard to produce a true sliding halt, because his conformation is not

right for it. The hardest thing I found at first was to teach her
to hold a slow Western jog, for it is never asked for in English
work. All Western paces are slightly different, consisting of
the walk, which should be active and ground-covering but not
hurried; then the jog, which is much slower and more relaxed
than an English trot, and therefore very comfortable for the
rider, who does not post in Western work. Next the lope,
which is also a smooth, ground-covering pace, and which a
horse can keep up for long distances without tiring, being
much less active than a collected canter. Western horses are
also asked to gallop on, but usually only for short distances,
to head off cattle, or when competing in Western Reining
classes, which are like very fast dressage events.

It took Don a few weeks before I could set her in a jog or
slow lope which she would hold until I asked her to change.
The other real problem was the flying change of lead at the
canter. I had taught her early in her training to do a counter-
canter for dressage, and now she found it almost impossible
to believe that I wished her to change leads without coming
back to a trot first. Most Western trained horses learn the
flying change naturally at the start of their training and are
able to do it to command. To this day Don finds the flying
change one of the most difficult movements to perform on
command, although she does it naturally when working fast
in the open. This was the last time I taught a young horse
counter-canter before getting a fairly good flying change out
of him first.

Having got all her paces established, I now began to teach
Don how to work a rope test and how to tackle the various
obstacles which may be met in a trail class. The rules of most
Western classes insist on a bridle being worn, but a bosal is
accepted. I discovered there was an Association in Britain
trying to encourage Western riding, called The Western Horseman's Association of Great Britain, which at this time had
about two hundred members and was centred around the
New Forest in England. Here farmers still run cattle loose in
the Forest, so there is an actual need for horses to be used in
the way the Western horse was meant to be used.

In the spring of 1972 I went south with Don and did a short course with one of the Western instructors, and took my Western Instructor's Certificate. This would enable me to teach Western riding in Britain, an interest and a need to me for I was now starting to run my stable as a riding centre as well as a stud farm, to cope with the rising costs in feeding.

I had taken the examination with Ann Hyland, who is a well-known teacher of riding and who recently published the book, *Beginner's Guide to Western Riding*. I became a member of The Western Horseman's Association and determined to go south to compete at some of their Western shows.

Plate 3.
Strathdon worked
equally well under
English or Western
tack, this picture
being taken at one of
our demonstrations.
See Chapter 11.

CHAPTER EIGHT

DURING the early spring of 1972 I had Don clipped out and fit, having done a few drag-hunts and two hunter trials without a bridle, all going well. As she was obviously a tough little horse, I decided to see how she would do in endurance rides, which were just becoming popular in this country. I increased her work to a steady two or three hours a day until she could easily cover thirty miles at seven miles an hour without taking much out of herself. We worked mostly in a Western saddle without a bridle and Don obviously enjoyed the work. I now wanted to qualify her for the Golden Horse Shoe Ride, which is the British Championship ride, run over seventy-five miles of very tough country.

There was a forty-mile qualifying ride held that spring in the south of Scotland and I entered it. The day was fine and clear with a reasonable breeze — almost perfect conditions except that it had rained for the whole of the previous week, which made much of the going in heavy mud. At the start I had an argument with the B.H.S. steward as to whether or not it was safe to allow me loose on the course without a bridle. After doing a few tests, including galloping another horse past Don, both while she was walking and cantering, and showing that I was still in perfect control, he let us start.

For the first half of the course Don gave me an excellent ride, which included negotiating a very narrow trail along a ledge for about a mile, with a high cliff above us and a sheer drop of about thirty feet to rocks and seashore below. On this stretch I was glad I was riding a sensible horse which I could trust; I know that many people had to dismount and lead their horses, but this is permitted in this type of ride. At the half-way halt Don passed the veterinary check, and after a compulsory half-hour's rest and a few short drinks, we continued on the second half. After about ten miles we came to a thick pine forest where men had been thinning trees and had left the branches strewn over the ground with no track between them. This enforced difficult, dangerous going, with a risk of horses cutting their legs on the sharp spikes. Conditions worsened where the ground under the branches was deep mud, sometimes coming up to the horses' knees and hocks. I hope I never have to ask a horse to go through such a terrain again. But now that we were in the forest there appeared to be no other way and I felt proud of my little horse while I made her go the way I wanted, and not once did she hesitate to go on plunging through this ghastly bog until eventually we came out on the other side of the forest. Knowing this bad stretch had taken more energy out of her than all the rest of the ride, I walked her for half a mile before having to push on to avoid incurring time faults.

At the end of the ride the horses were checked by the vets as they came over the finishing line, and again forty minutes later to test their recovery rate. Don and I got in well within the time limit and she was given 100 per cent vet points, thus qualifying us for the Golden Horse Shoe ride that year. Unfortunately, I was not to compete in it, for Don pulled a tendon in her hock while jumping, just before the big day.

After the ride I roughed Don off and gave her a month's rest while I got through the busiest part of the stud season. I was working three stud stallions that year. Having been roughed off at this time of year, Don was not ready for the Highland Show, but we competed in a few dressage and combined training events. Our successes were being placed in three classes at the Dryden event and winning the Novice Combined Training at the North East Riding Club event. I also did some show jumping and she went well, but at this stage I did not want to push her for speed, so we were usually unplaced.

In July I went south to Cambridgeshire for my first appearance at a purely Western show, held at Fengate, near Brandon, with all types of Western classes, both in hand and under saddle. I was to make many good friends in the Western circle because at this stage there was very little cut-throat competition in Western riding. I stayed with friends of the show's organiser, Mrs Sheila Parrott.

The show day was very hot and the ground exceedingly hard. The standard of Western riding varied greatly in those days, as did the dress and type of horse which was used. Not all the tack was Western – everyone was there for enjoyment. One rider stuck out strongly among the rest, Western riding obviously coming naturally to her. She was riding a striking pure Arabian grey gelding called Argosy and was an American from Nebraska, Dr Marjorie Barr, with whom I was to become firm friends in the future.

The ridden classes got under way with the Novice Pleasure Horse class, which is judged like an English hack class. The horses have to walk, jog and lope in each direction, showing a smooth action, steady head carriage and good balance on a loose rein. After the first line up each horse is judged for conformation and suitability for the job and his rider, and then they can be asked to give an individual display, probably including a figure of eight at lope and a stop and rein back. In this class Don was pulled in third in the first line up, and, much to my delight, moved up to first after the individual show. This was where we stayed. Marjorie Barr was no longer a novice and therefore not in this class. The next class was Open Pleasure Horse, judged on the same lines, but open to all horses. Marjorie won this one with Don second. Things were certainly going Don's and my way! The next class was Versatility, where all the horses come in and are judged first under Western tack and way of going, and then we are given three minutes to change tack and clothes inside the ring, to English gear. We are then judged again under hunter rules, including jumping, and the final scores are added together. This was Don's best class at this stage because of her good grounding in dressage and jumping and she won it easily.

The only other class I entered that day was the Trail class, where the horses have to negotiate various obstacles, such as walking over a bridge or down a row of tyres on the ground, backing through an "L" shape of straw bales or poles on barrels, drag a log forward and backward on a rope from the saddle horn, allow the rider to pick up a bag or bucket from the ground without dismounting, ride or be led over a jump, load into a trailer, and allow the rider to put on a slicker while mounted. Don went well, but knocked over one of the barrels and we finished in third place. Altogether I was very satisfied with our first venture into Western Showing, especially as the entries in each class had been large. The next day we went on to a smaller show with Western classes, and Don won three out of the four events, but the standard was not very high.

We had one more successful visit south to a Western show in Surrey, before the British Championships, and by now I was beginning to have hopes that Don might do well in the Novice Pleasure Horse Championship event. However, there were two Western horses in the country which I had not yet met, and I was looking forward to seeing them because everyone spoke so highly of them. One was Ann Hyland's Jacobite, who was almost a Quarter Horse, and was imported by Ann from America. The other was the previous year's Western Champion, Rabalain, a pure bred Arabian stallion, also imported from America.

Having entered for the Golden Horse Shoe ride, which was to be held at Goodwood, I was able to stable there for the Western Championships, being held nearby on the next day. Although I did not take part in the ride that year because of Don's injured tendon, already mentioned, I gained much valuable experience for future rides by watching how it was run, and seeing Ann Hyland win a Silver award on her Arabian stallion, Nizzolain.

The next day I drove to Surrey for the Western Championships and was at last able to see Rabalain, a beautiful little horse. Don had now qualified for both the Open and Novice Championships, and this year they decided to run the Open class first, which is unusual. There was a big entry and I did not expect to do very well against many much more experienced horses. However, Don was on top form and has natural presence. She was pulled in second to Rabalain in the first line-up. In the individual show she went well, including good flying changes, and we moved up to first place, under an American judge. I could hardly believe it and I was even more delighted because Philip was there filming it, although he does not usually go to Shows except when time-keeping at B.S.J.A. events.

Having won the Open, I felt I should withdraw Don from the Novice Championship, but we competed in the Versatility class, where we were third to Rabalain, and in the Trail class, where we came fourth because Don jumped over the tyres instead of stepping through them. I had ridden in this class without a bridle at the request of the Secretary, as there are no rules on tack in a Trail class, and he thought the people in that area would be interested to see it. Thus ended our first season in Western showing, which later proved to be a natural element for Don.

CHAPTER NINE

JUST after these events I had another unusual experience caused by making a horse a one-man animal.

When we came home I thought Don needed a rest, for she had been kept fit and doing concentrated schooling for over eighteen months, with only a short rest after the endurance ride. I told the girl who worked for me to turn Don out next day in a good pasture with my geldings. When I came to the stable after breakfast the next day, Don was out, but running up and down the top fence, whinnying. I thought the girl had put her out on her own and was furious, but I discovered the two other horses were out with her and she was neighing for me! This was the first time I had been in this situation and I was not sure how best to deal with it. Obviously I could not always be tied to Don, so I must break her of this dependence on me and I ignored her calling. I admit it was very hard to resist her and she kept up this screaming every time I appeared in the farmyard which was in sight of her field, for three days. After this she appeared to give up and went away grazing. But if she heard me talking, as when I was lungeing other horses, she would rush back to the fence and whinny. Shortly after this I started to work a very wild, young grey filly called Carona, which disliked human beings. I stabled her in the next box to Don in the hope that Don would tell her that people were nice to know. But almost the opposite happened. Whilst I was handling this filly in sight of Don, Don developed a mad jealousy of her. When we turned the two of them out together, Don went for Rona and after a mad chase put her

over the wall and out of the field. At first I thought Don was
jealous because of the old gelding,Fingal, who was also in the
field. Accordingly, next day we turned the two mares out
together, with no other horse, but exactly the same thing
happened. I was never able to turn these two out together
again, although they had been in close contact before I started
working Carona.

This jealousy with me began to show itself in another way
too. If I was teaching in the school, Don was always well
behaved and ignored other horses as long as I rode her. If I
wanted to get on one of the other horses, either to demonstrate
something or to teach the horse a new movement, Don would
put her ears flat back and try to bite or kick the horse I was
riding if it came within her reach. Even now, if I go out on a
hack with someone else riding Don, she immediately takes a
dislike to my horse although one she normally gets on well
with. Since the episode with Carona, I take great care not to
show too much affection to any other horse while in sight of
Don.

CHAPTER TEN

FOR the past twelve years I had been breeding horses, having built up my stud from two pony mares, an injured T.B. and a semi-retired T.B. stallion called Rocket. I had been given this horse at the age of seventeen, to give him a good home, and in the next ten years he built up my stud until he died at the age of twenty-eight. During this time I had been producing very ordinary horses of mixed breeding, although in the later years I had been standing two other stallions as well as Rocket. The time came when I had accumulated enough capital to clear out all the ordinary stock and start specialising.

In Great Britain I thought there was a lack of good all-round riding horses although there was a great demand for them. Over the past two years, as recounted, I had become interested in the American Quarter Horse, this breed appearing to be so versatile. They are powerful but not heavy; they have great speed and quality but are very sensible, and, best of all, they have such good temperaments that small children can ride big horses and even stallions and still be in control.

Through John O'Neill and Marjorie Barr I had made contact with Quarter Horse Breeders all over the U.S.A., and in the autumn of 1972 I planned to go out there to see what I could get with very limited capital.

Philip and I flew out at the end of November, stopping off in New York to check on details with the shipping agents. When I had written to John about buying Quarter Horses, he had told me that he had got a new job in New Mexico where there were many ranches breeding Quarter Horses for working

cattle and racing. He also said he had a "super" young Quarter
Horse mare with him in Roswell, N.M., but very sadly had
had to leave Lady at livery in New York, and that she was
still not sound enough to do hard riding. So, when I was in
New York, I went out to see her in Waccabuc, and I thought
she had changed considerably. She was well fed and looked
after, but the people there simply did not understand her
individual temperament. They had tried to ride her and make
her accept an English bit, although they knew she had always
worked without one. They tried lungeing her in tight side-
reins, but she had fought them continuously until they gave
up. The result was that they did not like her and she had lost
her trust and affection for people. Never having mixed with a
crowd of horses before, she had become a bully and very
much the odd one out.

Philip and I flew to Florida, where we had friends. Although
now early December it was warm and we spent a few lazy
days swimming and lying on the beach. We heard of a large
Quarter Horse ranch inland from where we were and arranged
to go to visit it to see what they had. It turned out to be a
high-class establishment with some top-class horses of the
"Jaguar" line, including the Florida State Champion. They
had some good mares and foals for sale which were what I
was looking for, but I wondered if they would be tough
enough to stand up to the severe Scottish climate. Although
it was December, the horses were still grazing on lush grass
during the day and stabled at night in temperatures of over
70°. Another point was that I was looking for working stock
horses and in this part of the country very few of these horses
had ever been used to work cattle.

I left Philip in Florida and flew north to Scottsbluff,
Nebraska — a slight change from Florida! I was held up overnight in Denver because of a blizzard which prevented my
connecting plane from taking off, and eventually arrived on
a clear, cold day, with 65° of frost, in the local mail plane,
which was the only one flying into Scottsbluff in these
conditions.

I was met by a friend of Marjorie Barr's and spent a very

pleasant night with her and her mother, discussing horses and their place in ranch life over the years. Next day we drove sixty miles out into the prairie country to a small place called Broadwater, and about ten miles farther on we came to the Covalts' ranch. It is in an isolated position surrounded by rolling sandy hills, and from the top of a hill one can see the road running dead straight as far as the eye can see. The Covalts were a delightful couple, running a 10,000 acre spread along with their son Philip and his family, and with the assistance of neighbouring cowboys at round-up time. This was an interesting visit for me because it is one of the few places left in one of the most modernised countries in the world where farm life still revolves round the horses and the cowboy. One reason is that the land is of shifting sand and wheeled vehicles moving on the land cause erosion, except when everything is frozen hard in winter.

Because of these conditions there is very little cultivation and most ranches rear cattle by grazing them out on the open plains and grow some alfalfa hay by irrigating parts of the land, for winter feed. The Covalts at this time were raising 1,000 head of Hereford cattle and about 100 head of pure bred Quarter Horses, tracing back to some of the best working blood lines in the country. They were Weiscamp lines and mostly bred back to the very famous stud horse, Skipper W.

Here I was certainly going to find the toughness I was looking for, all the adult horses being run out on the range all year round. They are divided into three bands, each about forty mares and a stallion, and they fend for themselves almost entirely. During the winter when the ground is covered in snow they are given some hay, but very little according to our standards—about six bales of about half a hundredweight each band per day, and at this time of year the temperature here under the shadow of the Great Rockies was 40° below zero Fahrenheit.

Once the foals have been weaned, about November, they are kept in corrals and small pastures near the ranch house for about two years, where they get some grain in winter and are handled to get them used to men. At about two years old

they are either sold or, if they are good enough to be kept for
the broodmare band, they run out on a local part of the range
for another year. Then they are broken and taught all types
of ranch work, as well as being shown both in halter and
under saddle. None of the horses go into the breeding band
until they have done at least two years' hard work to prove
they are sound and have cow sense.

Mrs Covalt, who runs the horse side of the business, very
seldom sells any of the mares once they are in the breeding
band. But I was looking for mares in foal, and she had three
in-foal mares, two of them lovely buckskins, which were
being sold because they were too closely related to two of
the ranch stallions and had produced albino foals to the third
stallion, which was a palomino. The one I liked best was a
nine-year-old, Stacy Cash, which was fifteen hands, and I
had seen a very good stud colt of hers in the home corrals.
She was in-foal to the palomino stud, Mr Show Bars, so I
took the chance that this foal could turn out to be albino
and she was within my price range.

On the next two days I spent an interesting time going out
with Mr Covalt in an old open pick-up, taking hay out onto
the range to the herds, checking the horses and breaking the
ice on the big tanks at the windmills. Some days this ice was
up to four feet thick and once it was broken with an axe the
horses had to drink quickly before it would freeze over again
in about an hour. In the previous month there had been such
a blizzard no one had been able to get to the horses for ten
days, but these tough animals had survived by eating snow
and digging through it for the coarse prairie grass. Only one
foal had been lost that time—they very seldom lose any unless
a coyote manages to get a young or weak foal.

Mrs Covalt showed me the breeding records over the past
five years, which showed the stallions' fertility rate never
lower than 97 per cent, which is very good compared with
most studs I know in this country.

Having made arrangements to buy Stacy and for her to
travel to New York to meet a charter plane, I sadly had to
leave this remarkable family.

CHAPTER ELEVEN

I SHOULD have liked to have had the time to stay longer with the Covalts, as there was so much more I could have learnt from them about training and working Quarter Horses.

I left Scottsbluff to fly to Albuquerque and Roswell, via Denver, but it took us two hours' circling round the airport before we were allowed to land at Denver, and then we were told the airport was again closed, and the airline put me up in a local hotel overnight. Next day the weather had cleared and I continued my journey to Roswell, but managed to lose track of my suitcase in Albuquerque and had to go on without it. John and his elder son, Sean, met me at the airport, and that evening we had a long discussion on our various experiences with horses. This was the first time I had seen John since I watched him working without a bridle.

Things were going well for them in this new life; John was now in advertising and living in the heart of the Western horse country. He told me how he had found his new mare, Miss Bay Charger, known as Missy, who was now a four-year-old. She had been an excellent Quarter Horse in halter classes, but had got her legs scarred and the owner did not want her any more because he only kept her for showing. This was in New York and John had been able to buy her at a very reasonable price. He had taken her home and turned her out with Lady, with no trouble the first night. The next day he had brought them both into the barn and began to handle Missie in preparation for eventually breaking her. He had been working her in full view of Lady and, when he turned both horses out again, Lady attacked Missie and chased her through a fence and down the drive before returning to the barn. At the time John was furious, but he did not think much more about it and only had to keep them separated. However, when we compared stories, this behaviour was so similar to Don's reaction with Carona that we realised they were suffering from jealousy and wanted us to be one-horse to them as they were one-man to us.

I was looking forward to seeing Missie and was not disappointed when we went to her pasture next day. Although she had a thick winter coat, here was obviously one of the finest Quarter Horses I had ever seen. She had all the muscle power of the Quarter Horse and also showed tremendous quality, which is sometimes lacking in the breed, and she had the most beautiful, intelligent head. She was a deep bay, and although John had had her for only a short time she already showed a great trust and affection for him.

During the next few days I visited over a dozen ranches and saw a few hundred Quarter Horses, varying in quality and price from $200 to $250,000, many of them top Quarter racing stock, so not the type I was looking for. John and I made an interesting visit to the Santa Rosa stud farm, where the most famous quarter mile racing Quarter Horse stands. He is Go Man Go, twenty years old yet some of his track records were still unbroken. We saw over their stables for two hundred visiting mares, each box having its own exercising pen at the back. The whole place was fenced in eight-foot-high post-and-rail fencing, with the various paddocks being divided by a ten-foot track to prevent risk of infection spreading from one to the other. The horses on this farm are so valuable that they have their own full-time veterinary surgeon and a complete operating theatre on the premises. We also made a day excursion to the Ruidoso Mountains to visit the great Ruidoso Downs race track, where the richest race in the world is run annually for Quarter Horses. But it was a small ranch just outside town which had the best type of horses for my purpose. This was Hilltop Ranch, belonging to Pete Hatch, who also had land in Texas. He had a fine herd of real working stock horses and was prepared to sell. I now had to work out how best to use my remaining capital to get me started in Quarter Horses in Britain, bearing in mind that I did not know of a stallion I liked in Britain. If I bought two in-foal mares I would be all right provided one of them produced a stud colt, but not if I were stuck with only females. Finally, rather than risk all my remaining cash on one in-foal mare, I decided on a three-year-old yeld mare and a colt foal. Good stud horses were expensive once they were old enough for one to see their conformation, but young colt foals were cheap.

We went out to the big weaning corral and saw about two dozen colt foals and six of them had the breeding lines I liked. These were range-bred colts and untouched by man, so in a driving snowstorm Mr Hatch drove them through a narrow chute while I tried to see how they moved. I at last decided on a dark chestnut which was fairly lanky but well made and appeared to have natural presence. He was a son of Dude Lit, which is by the well-known horse, Blonde's Dude, and was called Tuffy Dude.

Before finalising my plans to buy these horses I asked John if there was any chance he would ever want to sell his Missie, but he replied that if he could help it no amount of money would ever buy her, because he had already built up a close relationship with her and was working her bridleless. We also discussed Lady, and John was worried about her but did not know what to do. Having had her all her life he would never sell her, but if I thought it was worth the import costs and I promised never to sell her, he would like to give her to me for breeding. Having first learnt bridleless riding with Lady and then spent ten days nursing her after her foot injury, I thought a lot of this independent character of a mare. She had a great deal of quality although she was not pure bred, and I said I would love to have her.

Next day Philip joined us at Roswell and we made the final arrangements with Mr Hatch for travelling his two horses, Smoke's Honey and Tuffy Dude, to Scotland, a journey of about five thousand miles. While there we were interviewed by a reporter from the local paper about our plans for Quarter Horses in Britain and, considering it was done inside a barn with a howling gale going on outside, quite a good article made the front page of the *Roswell Times* next day.

The horses had to go through blood and other tests and could not travel with us, so Philip and I flew on to California. Here we spent a few pleasant days with a friend and his family on a big ranch near Paso Robles. I went out trail riding with his daughter and we all visited many local places of interest before flying back to New York. Arrangements were made for travelling Lady, as all my horses were to go to Kennedy Airport together, flying to London on a chartered plane, which is much cheaper than regular flights.

We arrived at Prestwick, and home, after a month's travelling covering 17,000 miles. The horses arrived safely in London at the end of February, very little the worse for many days of travelling by truck, plane, and then in my truck to Scotland, to start the first breeding herd of Quarter Horses in Scotland. Seven weeks later Stacy produced a lovely bay filly and she was appropriately named Luck Penny. There was already in Britain a horse called Tuffy Doo, so I registered Tuffy Dude as Waccabuc, which is a Red Indian name meaning Head of the Lake.

By now Don had had over two months' rest since the show season, and I started to get her up again and clipped her out. The Golden Horse Shoe Ride was being held in May in 1973 and I did not think I could make it, being in the middle of the stud season. I worked mainly on Don's dressage and some cross-country runs, as a change for us both. These runs are like drag-hunts, being run over an approximate ten-mile course which has been prepared beforehand, going straight across country so far as possible, jumping all walls, fences and ditches en route. They are generally run fairly fast and, to be enjoyable for the rider, require an obedient, good jumper. As these events take place in winter, the weather is often ghastly. I remember one day I went out on Don in a howling gale and driving sleet and I decided we were both mad! However, it was a good course and we had a great run in spite of the weather. On returning to my truck I untacked Don and rugged her up well with an anti-sweat rug under a thick blanket, and then I realised I was soaked through. It was already almost dark and I crawled into the cab of the truck, peeled off my sodden riding breeches and wrapped myself in a spare horse rug before starting up the engine. All was well until I was stopped a few minutes later by a farmer who said the road ahead was flooded and I would have to take a different route. As I did not know the area he suggested that I should come up to his house and he would show me the way on a map. It was not until I felt the rain on my bare legs that I realised I had flung open the door and jumped out wearing only a jumper, my underpants and riding boots. Before the farmer could say anything I retreated hastily and reappeared wearing the horse rug as a skirt.

During that winter I travelled Don to Edinburgh fairly frequently to compete at indoor combined training events. We won two of these classes and I found that jumping without a bridle has an advantage indoors because you can hold your horse out to the wall on all corners while still having her looking inwards, and so correctly bent for the next jump.

These indoor events prepared us well for the summer activities, and Don did some excellent dressage all over Scotland, winning the North East Riding Club's Novice Combined Training Class, and coming second in the Elementary Dressage event. She was well-placed again in three classes at Dryden, including our first attempt at a Medium test, which is the highest standard at which one can compete in Scotland.

Having got Don to a fairly high standard in Riding Club events, I decided to try for the open classes and entered her for the Spiller's Combined Training Competition in Aberdeen. This is a qualifying round for the Championships at the Horse of the Year Show, held each autumn at Wembley, which meant a number of entries from the south. Don did a fairly good dressage test and was lying fifth at the start of the jumping phase. Whilst I was working her over the practice

jump, a lady from the south came up and said, "Surely you
are not going to compete on her without a bridle at this
standard?" I felt like replying in the same sarcastic tone, but
had learnt by now that it was better to ignore such comments.
The jumping was over a fair course ending with an awkwardly
spaced combination, and the ground was very hard. I left the
pace entirely up to Don and she did a very steady round, to
produce the only CLEAR round that day! We did not, in the
event, qualify for Wembley, as her dressage was not quite
good enough; we had ended up third and only the winner
qualifies. I hoped my sarcastic rival, who also did not qualify,
might think again on the necessity of bridles.

Our next expedition south of the Border was back to the
Western Show at Fengate, Cambridgeshire. This year they
were including pure bred Quarter Horse classes in their inhand
section. During the spring I had broken the four-year-old
palomino filly, Smoke's Honey, and had been surprised how
easy it was — she seemed to want to do anything that was
asked of her. It took little over a week and she obviously
enjoyed being ridden. I had her working well without a bridle
in less than a month, but I did not feel she had potential in
this direction as she lacked sensitivity.

In the past six months Waccabuc, now known as Buck, had
passed through a very rangy stage, but by mid-summer he was
filling out and becoming a good-looking young horse. Don
and I set off south taking the two young Quarter Horses with
us, on their first public appearance. This time, having more
than one horse, I stabled them with a farmer, Henry Depford,
who lived in March, not far from Fengate, and I stayed with
Marjorie Barr, who also lived in the same area. This began a
long friendship with Henry and his family.

Once again this Show was to be a great success for our
stable. Buck started off by winning the young stock class
and then the overall Championship, beating all the adult
horses including three mature stallions. It was a great thrill
for me as it proved my venture into Quarter Horses had gone
in the right direction. The ridden classes followed fast and
Don won the Open Pleasure Class, and, much to my surprise,

Smokey won the Novice Pleasure Class. This left me in a dilemma as I obviously could not ride two horses in the Championship. I had seen Henry before at some of the Western events and knew that he was a good rider, so I asked him if he would like to ride Smokey for me. I also suggested that he ride her in the trail class as well; with her calm temperament I did not think a strange rider would upset her. Henry was pleased to have a ride, even on a young horse, for his own mare was lame. He got on so well with Smokey that he won the Trail class, beating Don and twenty other horses. In the Championship, which is usually the last event, he also did well and brought Smokey in as Reserve Champion to Don, beating a couple of American trained horses.

I had to hurry home after the show to prepare Don for a display of Western and bridleless riding which I had been asked to do at the Aberdeen Summer Show. Considering there were three other things going on in the ring at the same time, which was rather distracting for the horse, it went off quite well. This was our first public display working without a bridle and it produced an interesting response. Through it I met a few Americans now living in Aberdeen in connection with the North Sea oil drilling. They had taken special notice of us because I was using the first Western saddle they had seen in this country. Most of them were pleased to see someone doing Western riding in Scotland and were impressed by the control shown without a bridle. One man, however, was furious, saying I was making fun of the oldest style of horsemanship, as he had never seen a "cowboy" riding without a bridle. I guess you can't please everyone!

Shortly after this we had the great honour of being asked to join in a display of Western riding being organised by Ann Hyland for the Western Horseman's Association at the International Arab Performance Show. This is an important Show, held on Salisbury race course, and all horses taking part must be at least registered partbred Arabs. Ann was going to show a fast reining pattern and some rope work, followed by a quadrille of Western riders. Finally Don and I would show the slower paces and movements, working bridleless, and, we hoped, proving to the English riders, most of whom considered Western riding to be wild and furious, that it was neither rough nor required severe bits or spurs. Don went beautifully and I think the whole display was a great success.

Being at the Show anyway, I entered Don in the Working Hunter Class without a bridle, the catalogue saying that the type of bridle was optional. She went clear in the jumping and showed well, but her conformation was not top hunter standard. She also went well for the judge, with a bridle. He admitted that he had been wondering what he was going to do when it came to riding my horse and he was relieved when he saw my assistant produce a bridle for him. Don ended up fifth in a strong class. We had had a good day and made many new friends among the people who came to speak to us after the display.

CHAPTER TWELVE

THAT summer proved to be very hectic. No sooner had we returned from Salisbury than we were off again. My poor family have to be long-suffering during the summer months, but luckily I have a competent girl who looks after the house and the twins when I am away. And I could not lead the life I do if I did not have a very patient husband and a wonderful mother who lives less than two miles away from us and is prepared to help wherever needed: shopping, children or horses, she is always prepared to stand in for me.

We next went down to Hampshire to the Western Championships again; this year being held earlier, in August. Once more I had Buck and Don, plus a three-year-old I had just broken, called Shara, and they were all in good form. Buck won the Quarter Horse young stock class and then came Reserve Quarter Horse Champion, to a recently imported stallion, Bert's Reed, who was a lovely little horse.

The standard in the ridden classes was much higher than in the previous year, but Don's work had also considerably improved. She went well in the Pleasure Horse Championship and won it, to become the first horse to win it twice running. She came second in the Stock Horse Class, third in the Trail Class and first in the Versatility Class, thus gaining the High Point Championship. I had ridden the young mare, Shara, in the Novice Class and she had done well for her first outing, after the initial excitement, to come third in a big class, which was won by a fine Quarter Horse mare, with Ann Hyland's Nizzolan second.

This ended another successful year in Western events, but the season was not over for Don. I had decided to enter for one of the Endurance Horse and Pony Society's competitive trail rides, which was to be run over a forty-mile course on Dartmoor in October. She was already half fit with all our showing activities, so six weeks of long steady work, covering up to twenty-five miles a day, had her really hard and fit by the end of September. The drive down to Devon in the truck was in itself a feat of endurance. I picked up Ann Hyland and her young horse, Katchina, on the way and we eventually found the ride base at Headland Warren Riding Centre, after driving over miles of tiny, narrow, winding lanes, which are no joke in a six-ton truck.

The morning of the ride dawned dull and cold with a thick fog, and they had to delay the start for fear of losing the riders on the open moorland. By ten o'clock it had cleared enough and all the horses passed the vet check with no comments on Don's lack of bridle. Ann and I decided to ride together. As the mists cleared, both horses set out into the beautiful country in high spirits. For the first few miles I kept having to check Don and make her look where she was going, for she seemed to be far more interested in the new scenery around us than where she was putting her feet. When working without a bridle, it is amazing how much a horse likes to look around, especially when in new country.

We soon settled to a steady pace, aiming at doing nine miles per hour, to allow us to come in the last few miles slowly and so allow the horses' heart rate and breathing to settle before the vet check at the finish. The ideal speed to gain maximum points on this type of ride is six to seven miles per hour, not the fastest horse home, and the final results are decided on the horse's fitness and condition at the finish.

Much of this ride was over very steep and in some places very rough country and Ann and I did not stick together all the time. I know that, owing to having poor hocks, Don cannot keep up prolonged fast trotting. Wherever possible, I would canter on, then slow down, while Katchina was best at a steady, fast trot. We had some steep gullies and streams to cross and had to scramble over two of the famous rocky Tors, which added to the interest. Having ridden the ride to plan, Ann and I brought our horses in easily on time. Don came in with the best heart rate of the day, being 52, while her normal rate is 48, but, once again, her rather mad temperament came to the surface. We had walked the horses round until they were cool, unsaddled them and put them back to their boxes to await the final vet check, which takes place forty minutes after the horse has finished. Unknown to me, Ann went back to take Katchina out for his final and most important check almost ten minutes before I returned. Thinking she was missing out on something, Don had worked herself into a mad state of excitement and was charging round her box when I got there. The vet could not believe it; he told me later that Don had been points ahead of the others right up to the finish. Now, when her heart rate should have gone down to normal it had in fact risen to 72, which would normally indicate a very distressed animal, which was obviously not the case. I explained about her high-couraged, excitable nature, and he told me to put her back in the box with Katchina and he would check her again later. After twenty minutes she had settled down to normal but had to lose points for this, although it was not caused by exhaustion. This lost her first place in her first competitive ride, but she was awarded second place, and we had both had the enjoyment of the ride.

On our return home I once again roughed Don off for a rest, and this time she accepted it easily although she did not always enjoy being out of work.

I had by now got Stacy and Smokey in foal to a little horse in Yorkshire called Side Hill. I had also been working Lady lightly through the summer to try to harden her up a bit for foaling, for she had been out of work for two years. She had been covered by my grand old thoroughbred stallion, Windyedge, and she was becoming her old self again. Although the few weeks of stupid treatment in New York had ruined four years of hard schooling and I don't think she will ever return to the beautifully schooled horse she was when I first

knew her, she was recovering. She had recognised my voice at
London Airport and whinnied before she could even see me,
which was very pleasing. However, during the first week at
Manar she obviously pined, although the other Quarter Horses
settled in immediately. Lady always seemed to be looking
for someone, and the first real sign of pleasure she showed
was when my boys, then aged three and the same age as the
O'Neill boys, came up to the stable, when she whinnied to
them. She had always loved children and my Sean developed
a real relationship with her and used to spend hours sitting on
her while she was being grazed in hand during the quarantine
period, when the new arrivals were not allowed out to pasture.

That winter passed quietly and as it was an open one I
caught up with my routine jobs, like handling foals and
breaking youngsters, whilst continuing the schooling of the
young mare, Shara. When I bought her in the spring of 1973,
it had been with the intention of using her mainly as a student
horse. She was fifteen hands, grey, partbred Arab by the
Arab stallion Mikshara out of a partbred mare. She appeared
to be very suspicious of everyone and inclined to panic at the
least unexpected movement, but I thought this was just her
age. However, it turned out to be a very strong characteristic
of her temperament and made her breaking very difficult. I
worked her on similar lines to Don in the hope of gaining her
complete trust, but this was not so easy as she had a strong
inclination to resist a command without any reason.

I never properly gained the complete at-oneness with Shara
which I now had with Don, but by the winter of 1973-74
I was able to work her at home without a bridle, including
jumping. I think I could have done displays and other exercises
because she always ultimately obeyed me, but I was afraid
that in an emergency she would panic and ignore my aids.

CHAPTER THIRTEEN

EARLY in 1974 I started getting Don fit again because I had decided to have another "bash" at the Golden Horse Shoe Ride, though it was being held in the spring. This year was to prove Don to be one of the most versatile horses I had ever known, because of the number of different things she was able to do in a very short space of time.

By the end of January I was doing fifteen-mile rides at seven miles per hour and covering about fifty miles a week, increasing the distance through February. Having decided to try for the big ride on Exmoor I had to qualify for it again first. I entered a forty-mile qualifier which was being held in Leicestershire at the end of March. Although it was nearly five hundred miles away, Don is a good traveller. I made the journey the day before the ride and stayed with some people at Newseat Abbey.

The day of the ride was sunny and hot, which is a disadvantage for Don with her Clydesdale breeding, for she sweats very easily. However, we passed through the vet check and the judge accepted the fact that I rode without a bridle, after giving me a couple of tests to prove that I was in control.

We set out at a strong, steady pace which we were able to keep up throughout the ride without any problems. Don and I thoroughly enjoyed the ride in new country and she passed the half-way and final vet checks with full marks, having kept up an average speed of seven miles an hour which was good enough for us to qualify. Next morning Don was fresh and able to give our hosts a brisk jumping demonstration bridleless, before we set off for home. Apart from a puncture and a short engine failure on the truck, which did not appear to be as fit as Don, we arrived home safely, having picked up a visiting brood mare on the way.

After about ten days' lay-off, I started building up Don's work again, between the hectic routine of the early stud season. By this time I had been doing a certain amount of teaching riding professionally, to increase the income of the stud. Although it was very trying it gave me some interesting and amusing conatcts.

Most of my early customers came through the American Wives' Club, which is attached to the Oil Companies working off the north-east coast. Many of them would have been safer on bicycles and one good lady, who wanted to help, put the bridle on by hanging the rings of the bit round the horse's ears. But they were fun to work with and keen to learn, and always very appreciative of anything one did for them. Whatever side of equitation one takes up, it should be done because it is a pleasure for one reason or another. These ladies took up riding for pleasure and they loved to be out in the countryside watching nature through the seasons.

Regular customers came for long periods, riding once or twice a week, but one morning I had a phone call from a well-known stage actor. He said he had heard that I taught Western riding and that he wanted to learn it, for in a short time he was playing the lead in a pageant of Jesse James. The pageant would be out of doors at the Edinburgh Festival and he had to ride across the set at a gallop at least three times, riding Western and coming to a fast halt. He believed that anything worth doing was worth doing well, which was why he had contacted me. I began to suggest that we arrange a course of six lessons over the next ten days or so because I thought I could set him in the right direction in that time. He interrupted me to say that he was leaving this area for good the next day! I was rather taken aback but said I could take him that afternoon for a couple of hours to see if I could help him.

He arrived at 2 p.m. and I worked him hard on my seven-

teen hands hunter, Fingal, which was the only horse I had
that was schooled Western, but steady enough not to be upset
by an absolute beginner. I am glad I was not around when my
client got out of bed the next day. He had admitted not being
on a horse for at least ten years, but that afternoon he spent
two hours at a sitting trot on a very big horse. But he was a
natural athlete and had a feeling for animals and got on
surprisingly well. I think he may have looked quite professional
on the day, provided the Company managed to find a horse
who understood basic Western aids.

Plate 4. Strathdon jumping cross-country in Ireland. See Chapter 17.

63

CHAPTER FOURTEEN

ALL through April I built up the speed and distance I rode Don each day, and in the first ten days of May I did two long rides on consecutive days. The first day we covered forty miles going strong, and the next day we did twenty miles with no problems. This was my rehearsal for the Golden Horse Shoe Ride. The next week I let up a bit, just keeping Don ticking over on full rations, but not doing enough to cause stress. Owing to it being in the middle of the stud season I had to leave our departure for Exmoor, where the 1974 ride was being held, as late as possible. This was tough on Don, but she was used to it. On 14th May Wendy, one of my grooms, and I packed into the truck everything I could think we might possibly need.

At 6 a.m. on the 15th we loaded up and set off on the first leg of our seven-hundred-mile haul to Exmoor. Everything went well and we covered the 350 miles to Leeds in eleven hours. We were staying with a friend I had met on the Leicester ride, Carol Cotton, who was also doing the Golden Horse Shoe Ride. We unloaded Don and settled her in to a roomy box, for half an hour while we had tea. Then Carol and I took her mare, Shanta, and Don out for a short hack to supple Don up after the long hours of standing in the truck. Don settled in satisfactorily and Wendy and I stayed the night with Carol and her husband, John.

Next day we were up at 5 a.m. and left by 7, to drive to Taunton. There was a hair-raising hour getting through Birmingham. I had no idea where we were going and I was following John's car, but in the early morning rush hour we kept getting separated at road junctions. However, we managed to catch up again and finally got out into the open country roads once more. On arrival at the race stables where all the Ride horses were being accommodated, we unboxed, settled the horses in and went to find our caravan. Needless to say, it was at the opposite side of the race course from the stables, which was going to mean a great deal of carrying to and fro. I was also worried about Don's reliance on me, as she likes to know I am just round the corner and it was not so easy to keep popping out to see her from half a mile away.

Although we had arrived later than most other competitors, Carol and I decided to give our horses another short hack before presenting them for the pre-ride vetting, which is a very thorough test to decide whether or not the horses are fit to do a ride of this distance. Luckily both our horses passed the test but I had a disappointing argument with the stewards, who had decided that I would not be allowed to ride the course without a bridle. I still think this was a most unreasonable decision, taken without any consideration being given to the standard of the horse's schooling and degree of control. Don concentrates so much more on the track when working bridleless. I had ridden all previous rides, including the qualifiers, without a bridle, not to mention horse trials and speed events, but they would not alter their decision and I compromised by saying I would use a bosal hackamore. I was also riding Western, in an American "light ride" saddle over two pads, which the stewards described as a "bed roll", but to which they appeared to have no objections.

Next morning we fed the horses at 5 a.m., had breakfast, collected all our equipment, spare tack, first aid and all other requirements for horses under stress, and put it into John's car. Then we had to load up the horses and drive them twenty miles over steep, winding roads to the start at Watton Hall. It was a sunny day and going to be hot, which might cause problems with Don.

Carol and I set off together just after 9 a.m. and it proved to be a very tough, steep course over beautiful countryside,

if one had had the time to admire it. In the first fifty miles
we climbed from sea level to over 2,000 feet and back again
no less than seven times. Many of the slopes were so steep
that some of the riders had to dismount and lead their horses.
However, I felt safer on top of Don and stayed there, except
where it was uphill and too steep to make any speed; then I
walked to give her a rest and save her energy for the faster
parts. Although we started out together and made Gold speed
to the half-way halt on the first day, Don proved to be faster
than Carol's horse. At half-way there was a compulsory thirty
minutes' halt and two vet checks, during which time we tried
to make the horses drink salted water to prevent dehydration.

After the check Don and I rode out before Carol and,
sadly, Carol's mare pulled a back muscle shortly afterwards
and had to retire. All through the ride, John and Wendy met
us at intervals with water and sponges to wash the horses
down, and this certainly helped their comfort if not their
stamina. This was the first time I had pushed Don over a full
fifty miles, and, considering the severity of the course, I did
not yet know the limit of her endurance. At the three-quarter
mark I slowed her pace, aiming to come in on a Silver speed
of eight miles an hour but with top veterinary marks. Over
the last ten miles, both horses with which I had been riding
dropped out, and Don became very tired and disheartened.
Unfortunately it is impossible to tell a horse she has only six
more miles to go, but I got off and walked for a couple of
fields and kept her going slowly. This worked and we got into
base on my planned time and, I am glad to say, gained full
vet points for that day.

Ann Hyland, one of the best-known Endurance riders in
Britain, and now on her third G.H. Ride, had done a good
ride on Nizzolan to come in on Gold time of nine miles an
hour and full vet points. She remarked the distance seemed
greater than it was meant to be.

As soon as Don was cooled off enough to travel I loaded
up and set off over some terrifyingly steep hills and single
track roads to pick up Carol and poor Shanta. Although she
was stiff, the mare was not distressed and we soon had both

horses back at the stable and settled for the night. Don did not eat much of her morning feed, but she had cleaned up all the night one and rested well. She came out fresh at the 7 a.m. vet check and was passed sound. Shanta was obviously out of the ride but John and Carol said they would come over to the course and support Don and me on the final stretch.

I started the second day's riding with Brian Shepherd on a palomino stallion, who was also aiming at a Silver award. This day's course was also over very steep country, but the day was cooler, if wet, and our horses made the twenty-five miles easily. The worst part was the terrible rain, which turned the moorland into a bog and made it very tough on the horses to try to keep up the speed required. Brian's horse and Don paced each other well, but the more cobby stallion kept up a strong trot whilst Don, owing to her poor hocks, had to canter most of it. On one slope I had to hang on round Don's neck to stay in the saddle as she slithered and scrambled up the last mile to the finish. Brian and I crossed the finish line together and passed the vet check with top marks. We now boxed back to the race course and cleaned up ourselves and the horses ready for the presentation of awards.

There were ten Gold winners, including Ann and Nizzolan, six Silvers, including Don, and eight Bronzes. As soon as we got everything packed up, John and Carol had to dash back to Leeds to look after their family. Out of consideration for the horses after such a hard couple of days, I took them to Ann Hyland's place for the night and set off for Leeds the next day.

CHAPTER FIFTEEN

DON was now an eight-year-old and doing a variety of strenuous activities, and I decided this would be a good year to take one foal from her to get her started in breeding. A mare which reaches her teens without having had a foal is often very difficult to get in-foal later. I knew I would never sell Don and would want to breed from her. At this time I owned two thoroughbred stallions as well as my good young Quarter Horse, and I thought that this period of rest after the Golden Horse Shoe Ride would be a good time to get Don covered. However, Don had other ideas. Soon after the ride she showed in season and I tried to introduce her to my big T.B. MacRocket, but she attacked him on sight. It was a most unnatural reaction, for she appeared to be very much ready for a horse when she was at least fifty yards away from Rocket, but as soon as she got within touching distance she put her ears flat back and went for him with her teeth. After the first of these attacks, Rocket retaliated by going for Don with his teeth and front feet, and it was quite clear we were not going to get a successful service.

Over the next few days we tried all the usual methods of persuading a mare to accept a certain stallion, but even with the help of the vet and injections nothing worked. Rather than miss her I turned her out to run with my old T.B. stallion, Windyedge, a perfect gentleman, always lives out with his mares and has often got difficult ones covered. However, he was terrified of Don and although they ran together for over a month he would not even attempt to

cover her. During this time the vet had given her various tests
and decided she was a non-breeder and we might as well give
it up as a bad job.

After her rest I started schooling Don for the usual summer
activities, including Western events, and she began to learn
the rope test to perfection. About this time I met a couple
from America, the Webbers, who came out to see all my
Quarter Horses, and this was the start of a very happy friendship. Rosa Webber helped me polish up some of Don's Western
schooling. She had shown frequently in America before they
had come overseas with the oil company.

Our first big event that summer was the Northern Combined
Training event, which again included the Spiller's qualifying
round for Wembley. Don's dressage is never her strongest
point and she was only sixth after that phase, but a good
clear round in jumping brought her up to third. However,
she was still not good enough to qualify.

At the end of June that year we set off on one of the most
interesting trips to come out of my work in this type of
training. I had been invited to be the entertainment attraction
at the three-day show being held at the Old Court Equestrian
Centre, Kilkenny, Eire. I had my doubts as to whether we
were up to the standard they expected, for they had had
some Russian Hussars the previous year.

I worked out an effective hour's programme, starting with
Don demonstrating correct Western work with a bridle, then
taking the bridle off and continuing with very fast movements
like the sliding halts and rope test. While my assistant changed
Don's saddle to an English one, I did a few simple movements
on my two-year-old Quarter Horse stallion Waccabuc to show
the audience a true Quarter Horse. I followed this with a
demonstration of basic dressage movements, including lateral
work, on Don, bridleless, and finished with some jumping,
depending on what equipment was available.

Obviously I would have to make some type of explanatory
commentary, preferably given by someone who knew exactly
what I was doing, to keep the audience informed of what was
happening. I decided to take a friend along with me, and Jane

Pidcock, who was brought up in Ireland, joined the party, and saved some awkward situations on a few occasions.

We drove from Aberdeen to Liverpool with my big truck divided in half to give each horse plenty of space in which to move around. We boarded the ferry at six in the evening, watered and fed the horses and turned them loose in their half of the truck, as they had to remain in the truck all night. Typical of his breed, Buck quickly accepted the situation, ate up his feed and settled down peacefully for the night. Equally typical of her family, Don was furious. Because the truck had stopped she thought she should be immediately unloaded and put into a comfortable stable, instead of being left in the truck and surrounded by tremendous noises and the vibration of the ship's engines. She began kicking and banging the side of the truck soon after we boarded the ferry, was still doing so when Jane and I retired to our cabins at 11 p.m. and was at it when we got up at 5 a.m. to prepare for docking.

Before we left home, Mrs Martin, who owned the Old Court Equestrian Centre, had asked me if I could bring over some peanuts, as they were impossible to get in Eire and an elderly friend of hers loved feeding and watching tits through the winter. I had not realised how difficult the customs can be about foodstuff entering Eire and we had a hundredweight of peanuts stored under the tack in the luggage compartment above the cab. I knew we could not take any hay into the country and intended to throw any the horses had left over the side of the ship before entering port. This is what always used to be done on the old cattle boats, but on the ferry the trucks were parked underneath the passenger decks and the stewards would not let us through to dispose of our surplus hay. Being unsettled, the horses had left a considerable amount of hay and when the customs officials came aboard a great argument began. They said we could not come ashore with the hay on board, although we had not been told this before leaving England, and, moreover, they said we would have to stay on board and return to England with the ferry. I was furious. We had only one day before the show and I couldn't see why they wouldn't burn the hay on the quay.

All through this argument and the following veterinary
inspection I was terrified they would come across the peanuts.
At the beginning of the argufying I had forgotten about the
peanuts and now I felt they would not accept any explanation
for trying to smuggle even more foodstuffs into the country.
I hardly dared look at Jane, as she had difficulty in keeping a
straight face, being Irish, and obviously imagining my efforts
to explain having such a quantity of nuts on board a truck.

Eventually an obliging vet passed the horses and agreed to
burn the hay and we were allowed to continue our journey.

The Irish people were most kind to us and their first show
of hospitality came when Mrs Penny McAulay met us at the
docks and took us to her house for a bath and breakfast. She
was Penny Morton before marriage and had for many years
trained with Col. Dudgeon and used to give some wonderful
displays of riding without a bridle on a little African horse
called Corbus. Both of us having trained horses in such similar
work, although Penny had never competed without a bridle,
we had a great deal in common and had a very pleasant chat
over an enjoyable hot meal. We fed and watered the horses
and set off on the last leg of our journey to Co. Kilkenny.

After leaving the main road I began to wonder if we were
ever going to get there; the road became more and more
twisty, up and round steep hills and through tiny villages with
very narrow streets. When we came into Thomastown we
stopped a man in a picturesque little jaunting cart, and asked
him the way. Following his directions we found the sign to
Old Court, but had to reverse the truck three times to get
round the corner into the lane. We arrived to a great welcome
from Mrs Martin and all her staff.

Almost before Jane and I were out of the cab, her grooms
had the horses unloaded and into deeply bedded boxes,
bandages off and rugs changed. We had a delicious late lunch
and met the elderly Mrs Broadbent, who at that time was
confined to a wheelchair following an accident, and she was
delighted to receive our large bag of nuts for the tits. Later
we let the horses stretch their legs and saw over the smart
new centre which had been opened only that summer. We

then spent a very pleasant evening with Mrs Martin and Mrs Broadbent, and Jane, who had been brought up in this part of Ireland, caught up with the latest news of old acquaintances.

*Plate 5.
Mrs. Shuna
Mardon
jumping
Strathdon
without
a bridle.*

CHAPTER SIXTEEN

WHILE planning the event Mrs Martin had asked if I would assist in judging the Hunter Classes on the morning of the first day of the Show, our own first display not being until later. I had agreed happily, but you can imagine my horror when I found that the other judge could not come and I was landed with the whole job. Many of the horses were preparing for the Dublin Show and were, therefore, of top quality. The entries were also very big, there being nearly forty in the Lightweight Class. One point which surprised me greatly was that all but two of the horses were only four-year-olds.

While watching the horses I was puzzled that very few of them were asked to gallop on, although the conditions were perfect and the arena large. When I came to ride these big young horses, most of them well over 16.2 hands, I realised why — they had "no brakes"! Eventually I sorted them out, but not without upsetting at least one owner, and I was glad that my Supreme Champion went on to win his class at the Dublin Show.

Our first performance took place during the lunch break from Show events on the first day, and Don was in top form. Jane introduced us and kept up a continuous commentary, explaining the technical points of Western work and how I had taken up the bridleless work. I started off working Western with and without a bridle, as planned, showing the really fast work and how to teach a horse rope work, including dragging a barrel from the rope attached to the saddlehorn.

Then I gave Don to Jane to change saddles, while I mounted

Buck and jogged and cantered him round the ring to show
the people a pure Quarter Horse's movement and superb
temperament. Changing back to Don I continued with some
dressage movements, including shoulder-in and half-passes,
which Don loves doing as it always produces a round of
clapping. After the dressage we completed a round of show
jumping over a tough course.

Our audience gave us fair applause as the announcer asked
them all to move round onto the sloping hillside overlooking
the cross-country course. Although I had walked round the
ten fence course of about Riding Club Open standard in the
morning, Don had not seen any of the jumps before. As the
spectators sorted themselves out, I prepared Don for the
faster work. Having circled the first field at a fast canter, I
swung into the first fence at a good hunting pace. Then we
steadied up and turned sharp left up a steep hill and over an
awkward brush fence, which was the first element of an "in
and out" jump, through the corner of a pen. It was a tricky
jump so early in the course, but Don coped with it neatly,
jumping close and using her back to gain height. After this,
a good gallop to a straight wall into a wood and over some
hunt jumps, then back towards the start over a tiger-trap, a
sharp turn and a stile, followed by a good spread fence, and
so home.

This time the audience exploded into applause, and I later
discovered that they were so much more impressed by this
part of the display because they were nearly all hunting people
and found it very hard to stop, going cross-country, even
with a bridle. We repeated this display later in the afternoon
before settling the horses back into their boxes for the night.

CHAPTER SEVENTEEN

WE REPEATED our display outside again twice during the second day of the Show, but the biggest one was to come that evening in the new indoor arena, which had attached to it an up-to-date Clubhouse for the Riding Centre. Throughout the two previous days, Mrs Martin's house had been like a beehive, with a dozen or more local ladies rushing about preparing the buffet dinner for the opening ceremony for which they had sold two hundred tickets. There were whole hams and huge turkeys being cooked, dozens of loaves of bread being cut up and spread, and innumerable lettuces, tomatoes and other fresh vegetables being prepared as salads on huge platters. All the food was home-made and when it was finally prepared the tables looked most attractive, laid out along the big hall in the front of the Clubhouse.

During the earlier displays we had heard various comments, including remarks that Waccabuc's good behaviour was more credit to my horsemanship than to the good nature of the breed. In view of this, we decided that in the last display Mrs Martin would ride him; everyone knew her and would realise that she could not possibly have ridden the horse previously.

The gallery, which runs the full length of the Riding School, was full, and I wondered how Buck would react to such a large crowd indoors, but he took it all in his stride. Don loves being the centre of attraction and put on a very good performance. We followed our previous routine except for the cross-country section, which obviously had to be left out.

On a few occasions during the display there were some disturbances in the audience, but we thought it was a few lads who had been drinking and we carried on regardless. At the end of the display Buck went beautifully for Mrs Martin and impressed his audience, one of whom later offered to buy him for £3,000.

When we brought the horses back to the stables, two of the officials rushed up to Mrs Martin to tell her that they had at least fifty gate-crashers, who had got in by climbing over a high fence. They were causing chaos, grabbing far more food than they could possibly eat, wrecking the beautiful layout of the tables and breaking bottles, as well as being generally unpleasant.

Poor Mrs Martin was very upset, for this was the grand finale of the official opening of her magnificent new school and clubhouse, and the party was a way of thanking everyone who had helped in getting the venture off the ground. The Clubhouse was licensed until 4 a.m. and it was now only 11 p.m. The dance band had only just begun, yet there was trouble already. Mrs Martin went quickly to the Club and tried to talk to the trouble-makers, but they got very rude and threatened real violence. The barman, who was a local policeman, came to Mrs Martin and suggested he should close the bar at midnight, because he recognised some of the trouble-makers as supporters of the I.R.A. from north of the Border, which was only eighty miles away.

This plan was immediately agreed upon and with the help of a few more off-duty policemen, who were guests because they had been organising the traffic for the Show, the barman closed the bar, and after about an hour of scuffling got the place cleared, much to the disappointment of most of the guests. He organised a few policemen from the local force to keep a watch on the place for the rest of the night, in case the hooligans returned to finish their fun. However, all was quiet during the night, but it was a most disappointing end to what should have been a wonderful evening. The mess in the Clubhouse next morning had to be seen to be believed, but apart from a few broken windows there was no major damage.

CHAPTER EIGHTEEN

THE next evening Jane and I were invited to have dinner with
the MacCalmonts at Mount Juliet. We had a delightful evening
in one of the most wonderful houses I have ever seen. It had
been in the family for generations. An outstanding feature
was the ornate plastered ceilings in all the rooms. This was
the home of the Mount Juliet Stud, where the very famous
stallion, Tetrach, had lived all his life. The walls were covered
with portraits of this superb horse and offspring. I was
particularly interested in this stud, for my first stallion,
Rocket, was a grandson of Tetrach and his dam, Tetratema.
Tetratema had been carrying Rocket when she was sold from
Mount Juliet during the Second World War. Jane and I were
invited to visit the stud before leaving Kilkenny the next day,
which we did before packing up for home. It consists of three
large yards, each with stallion quarters, visiting mares' boxes
and foaling boxes. The foaling boxes are all built in pairs,
with a small observation room between each pair where the
stud groom on duty can sit and watch the mare through a
small window without her being aware of him. The well-
known stallion Sassafras was occupying the Tetrach's
quarters and he lives in a spacious loose-box about 15 feet by
15 feet, with an outside door opening onto the main yard,
and another one which opens into a large circular covering
box which can be used as an exercising yard in bad weather.
The establishment was as near to a stud owner's dream as I
have ever seen.

  That afternoon everything was packed back into the truck

and we said sad goodbyes to Mavis Martin and all our new
friends. We had an uneventful run back to Dublin and caught
the evening ferry for Liverpool. This time Don seemed to
accept the situation and settled down quietly for a peaceful
night in the truck. Next morning we disembarked, cleared the
customs with no worries, and set off for a rather boring run
home.

I gave Don and Buck a few days' rest before setting off
on our next excursion. I caught up on my routine jobs and
teaching, which is always neglected during the summer. At
this time my head girl emigrated to Australia and left with
very short notice. I did not have another experienced girl on
the place at that time, but Jane Pidcock very kindly came to
my assistance again. She was already an experienced horsewoman and knew my horses and it did not take long to show
her the running of my stable.

Having only one girl now working at home, I set off on my
own on 13th July for another long journey to Cambridgeshire
and the Fengate Show. I had a full load of four horses, as I
was taking Henry Depford's part Quarter Horse mare back
home. She had been to visit Buck, who had covered six mares
this year, but she stayed with us for three months and never
came into season. This was sad, for she was a very good type
of mare but too small for Henry and he had hoped to sell her
as a broodmare and buy a bigger Quarter Horse, possibly from
my stud. I also had with me my yearling Quarter Horse filly,
out of Stacy Cash, as well as Don and Buck.

We arrived safely and Henry helped get all the horses
settled in for the night before I went on to stay with the
Barrs, where we had a pleasant evening catching up on all the
horse news from opposite ends of the country.

The Fengate Show always seems to be a successful event
for my horses and this year Buck set the trend by winning
the Quarter Horse Championship in the inhand classes, with
my yearling Luck Penny coming fourth in an open class.
Many people were interested in Buck as a stud horse, and
three of them made bookings for the 1975 season.

Don was once more on top form and won the Open Pleasure

Class and the Stockhorse Class, although I forgot to tighten
my rear cinch on the saddle and nearly pulled myself and the
saddle off the horse when dragging a heavy log from the
saddle horn. Don also came second in the Trail Class and
finished by winning the Pleasure Horse Championship. During
this event I realised that Don had got herself right to the top
of this type of event in this country and I made up my mind
that if she won the British Open Pleasure Horse Championship
this year, which would be the third time running, I would
retire her from this type of competition. I consider a good
show animal should retire when at the top rather than go on
until it is beaten by a younger animal, and also that in a small
association it is bad for one animal to be always at the top.
Over the past three years she had proved her consistency in
Western work and her versatility in her ability to perform in
all types of events, with or without a bridle.

Marjorie Barr's Argosy did very well at the Show but was
too full of himself to gain top marks, as was Ann Hyland's
Nizzolan, which came Reserve Champion to Don. There were
one or two new Quarter Horses going well, including a strong
mare called Jean Darr, which had been used in an American
display team and was now owned by John Skelton.

The next day was more peaceful; cleaning the truck and
the tack and turning all the horses out to graze, because I was
staying in the district for a few days to be able to compete
at the East of England Show, which had decided to put on
Western classes for the first time this year.

The following day I took an interesting ride with Henry
round his farm, which is very different from ours. Owing to
the land being completely flat and almost on sea level, most
of the fields are divided by large drainage canals instead of
fences; it seems strange to look around for miles and see no
walls nor fences.

Being so close to London, the farm does not carry much
stock, but grows all kinds of market garden produce, such as
peas, beans and potatoes, as well as a large acreage of grain
and sugar beet. Henry showed me his father's show ponies,
which are outstanding, this small stud having produced some

of the most famous names in the country, including Pretty Polly.

The East of England Show is probably the third-largest all-round agricultural show in the country and when we arrived on the Thursday morning the ground was packed with spectators. I had only Don there because there were no Quarter Horse classes. She won the Pleasure Horse Class and was second to Argosy in the Stock Horse Class. She went extremely well in spite of the fact that the Royal Marines were letting off smoke bombs over our heads from the next door arena.

The day was extremely hot and burst into a thunderstorm before the Western classes, and I arrived back at the Barrs' almost exhausted at 9 p.m. Then to my surprise I found it was Marjorie's sixtieth birthday party and immediately all the problems of the Show were forgotten. I scrambled out of my dirty riding clothes and into a cotton dress, there being no time for a bath. We had an extremely happy evening which stretched into the early hours of the morning.

Later that morning I packed up and set off on the long journey back to Aberdeenshire. The news on arrival was anything but good. Whilst I was away, vandals had come to the farm, opened seven gates and let my 17-hand T.B. stallion MacRocket in with the broodmares. Considering what could have happened we got off fairly lightly, but, as may be imagined, Rocket attacked the two geldings and tried to cover various mares and got himself badly kicked in the process. He had to have fourteen stiches in a big wound on his chest and had a considerable amount of smaller cuts. Luckily Rocket was unshod, and the geldings escaped with bruises and bites all over their bodies but no serious injury. It will always amaze me to think what possible pleasure anyone could get out of seeing animals fighting and being injured, but I can see no other motive for this act of vandalism. A week later a neighbour of ours found their horse so badly shot up by airgun pellets that it died of its injuries.

CHAPTER NINETEEN

BUCK, only a two-year old, was beginning to make a name for himself both as a good Quarter Horse and as a stallion with a superb temperament. Since the visit to the Fengate Show, two purebred Quarter Horse mares had been sent up, over five hundred miles, to visit him at stud. One of these was to stay here for the year and be broken in as well as to breed, and I realised that I was afraid I was not going to have time to do justice to all my different types of horses.

I now had two very good young stallions, the big thoroughbred MacRocket and Buck. They were so different in type and the purpose for which they were best suited that I decided I could not campaign them both successfully. I was just introducing the Quarter Horse to Scotland and trying to sell a completely new breed to the equestrian public; therefore I must concentrate on Buck, and I negotiated to lease MacRocket to a lady in Aberdeen. This was near enough for me to send my hunter mares to him, and I knew that the stud groom, having only the one stallion to work on, would produce him to the best advantage.

Once again Don showed her versatility by winning the Working Hunter class at the local show in this area, although she had to wear a bit; normally I never jumped her in one.

At this time I took a few days' break from horses to go to the west coast with Philip and the boys, where we have a small house. It is obvious that during the summer months my household revolves round horse events and, at the age of four, one of my sons once summed up my life very well. He and some of his pals at playschool were discussing the facts of life, including whom they were likely to meet again when they reached Heaven. After some thought Sean stated: "I don't think I will meet Mummy when I go to Heaven." Being rather surprised, the teacher asked him why and he answered immediately: "She won't have time, she'll be at a horse show!" Nevertheless, Sean is very interested in horses and I think will be competing at shows himself one day, although his brother, Keith, is much more interested in machinery.

After this short break I started work on Don in preparation for the Endurance Horse and Pony Society's competitive long distance ride being held at Dartmoor at the end of September. She was, of course, fairly fit from all her showing activities, but lacked the long steady work required for endurance riding.

A real surprise in Don's career came when I went to Yorkshire to do a demonstration of bridleless work and show the versatility of the Quarter Horses, using one of my broodmares, Smokey Honey, and another mature stallion from Yorkshire, Side Hill. We were staying with the Keebles, who own Side Hill, and had been there before as Smokey Honey now had a foal at foot by Side Hill, and I had stopped off there with Don on some of my previous travels.

As we unloaded in the yard, Don started whinnying to Side Hill and Peta suggested that she had fallen in love with him, but I told her of Don's reactions to stallions and we forgot the subject for a time. However, after they had been calling continuously across the yard to each other for nearly an hour, Peta persuaded me to take Don over to speak to Side Hill and see what would happen. I did so, expecting the usual fireworks, but to my amazement she encouraged his attentions as hard as she could. Side Hill was certainly not the horse I would have chosen as a mate for Don, for he was small and very powerfully built, but it appeared that I did not have much choice in the matter if I wanted to get Don started in breeding. It was certainly a "love match" and she stood perfectly to be covered both that evening and the next day.

Our demonstration the next day at one of the agricultural shows was the most erratic one Don has ever done, as Side Hill was also in the ring. Although she never actually disobeyed me, she had three-quarters of her attention on Side Hill and a quarter on the job we were doing. The end of the display was a round of show jumping and Side Hill was standing just beside the last fence. I did not know whether or not she was going to jump till we were in the air.

We covered Don once more the next morning and then set off for home, with Don happily in foal as it turned out later. When I informed the vet of the situation, he said he would believe it when he saw the foal on the ground, as nature did not work that way!

For the next two weeks Don and I kept up the long distance rides and she was in great form and went very well in any Western schooling I did in between. I did all the endurance work, even on main roads, without a bridle because she works so much better this way, but I had to do some school work with a bridle to keep her in practice for the shows.

CHAPTER TWENTY

BY THE time we came to leave for the 1974 Western Championships, Henry Depford had decided to buy Smokey's foal, Smokey Mountain, and we were able to take them both down with us. At Henry's place we spent the night and weaned Smokey from her foal without much fuss. Next day I went on with Don, Smokey and the three-year-old Shara, and stayed with Ann Hyland, the Show being held in Hampshire again.

It had rained continuously for a week in that area, and on the morning of the Show there were heavy gales and we were held up twice on the way to the Show by blown-down trees on the road. Conditions at the Show ground were absolutely ghastly, with mud in the main ring so deep it came up over the horses' fetlocks. In spite of the conditions and with violent squalls of rain throughout the day, Don put on her usual showy performance and completed her last Western Show as a real Champion. She was unbeaten in four classes, varying from the Pleasure event to the Working Stock Horse class, and so achieved the record of winning the British Pleasure Horse Championship for three years running.

Buck also kept up his good record and won the 1974 Quarter Horse Championship, judged on conformation, while being shown inhand. The young mare Shara went well for her first show and was third in the Novice Pleasure class. Smokey also showed well inhand, to come reserve to Buck, and she went well for Henry in trail and cutting, but was not placed this time.

The next day, of course, the weather was beautiful! Don and I went on a twenty-five-mile Pleasure ride with the Endurance Horse and Pony Society group from the New Forest. Mrs Resa Webber, who comes from New Mexico, and who had been judging the previous day, rode Smokey and enjoyed her first trail ride in Britain. Don was working bridle-less and caused a sensation, as none of the locals had seen her before and they were convinced that she would bolt and join the wild ponies in the Forest.

Resa drove north with me and we had one rather alarming incident when the engine of my elderly truck went on fire on the M6 Motorway. Resa leapt out and rushed to unload the horses, but the thought of two mares and a stallion on the motorway was more worrying to me than the fire. Knowing that diesel does not explode in the way petrol does, I switched everything off and attacked it with our small extinguisher, which soon put out the small flame, and the rest then cooled off in a short time. The cause had been a leaking fuel pipe and once the breakdown servicemen had replaced this we were on our way without having unloaded the horses.

After this Show I really had to get down to planning and marking the route for our endurance ride. I soon decided that I would not compete in it, becuase it would be too difficult to organise and ride in it at the same time. This was the first ride of this type in Scotland and no one else knew how it should be run, not even the vets who are actually the judges. The big day dawned exactly like the one for the Western Show—pouring rain and very high winds.

In spite of this the ride was not impaired. We had only five competitive entries, as it was such a new sport in Scotland and many people were afraid their horses could not cope with the twenty-five miles. However, all those which started completed it without any problems. We also ran a Pleasure Ride over half the distance to help bring in funds, and most riders seemed to enjoy this despite the weather.

CHAPTER TWENTY-ONE

DURING this summer I had backed Buck so that he learnt the basics of riding manners as well as working mares, and he proved to be a very intelligent, sensible young horse. After the hectic summer I now started to rough Don off and was able to spend some time with Buck, although he did only short rides because of his age. I also worked him loose in the indoor riding school and he loved to jump when loose. At this time I interviewed a pleasant girl for the stable and it looked as if we were going to have a more peaceful winter.

Then, suddenly, in the middle of November, I had a letter from John O'Neill telling me that the job in New Mexico had fallen through and that he was now living near Los Angeles in mountain country, and the nearest place he could keep Missie was eighty miles away. This was not a good situation either for him or the mare, and as he did not see much chance of the situation changing in the near future he offered to sell Missie to me. This came as somewhat of a shock, and at a very bad time for me. I had always liked Missie, but I had no idea that she would ever be for sale and therefore had not examined her from the point of view of buying her. Now I had to make up my mind quickly. Having been away so much all summer I had not intended making any movements for the rest of the year, let alone all the way to America!

Before deciding whether it would be possible, I phoned Lep, International Bloodstock Transporters, to see what it was now costing to import a horse. At this time I had no spare capital and realised that I would have to sell at least

two of my present horses before I could go ahead and buy
Missie.

Having given me the information I asked for, the agent
from Lep, who had known me for a long time and knew I
was very experienced with horses, asked me if I would be
interested in a free flight out to see the horse. I was very
surprised but certainly interested. He told me that his usual
crew on the Atlantic run were held up in Kenya. Because of
this he was short of knowledgeable grooms to go out with a
load of thoroughbreds from Gatwick to New York.

Of course I couldn't miss the chance, because I wanted to
see Missie again before taking the expensive decision to buy
and import her. However, I got another shock when the agent
said the flight was going out in three days' time! I did not
know if John would be at home at that time and there was
no point in going out, even on a free flight, if he were not.
I madly set about making plans but, although I was used to
making short-notice journeys, this seemed too much to arrange.
I cabled John to get him to send me his phone number by
cable, and then phoned him to make final arrangements.

During the next two days I organised various people to
look after my household and stables for the week I would be
away. I also, surprisingly, managed to lease an Arab broodmare of mine for five years, and sell a good young Quarter
horse mare, which just about gave me the capital I needed.

The grooms for the flight were told to meet at Gatwick
Airport at 11 p.m. on the Sunday to load up the horses for
a 3 a.m. take-off on the Monday morning. I took the train
to London and made my way to Gatwick, arriving at the
arranged meeting place behind the passenger terminal near
the cargo depot. It was a freezing cold night at the end of
November and I hung about for half an hour but there was
no sign of anyone possibly connected with horses. I found
a workmen's café in a nearby building and had a cup of
hot coffee and waited another hour.

The next time I checked round the cargo bay I was relieved
to find one lone horsebox parked there. The driver had been
warned that charter flights usually took off late but he did

think something should have been happening by now, as it was 1 a.m. Suddenly the agent for the charter company arrived and told us that loading was delayed until 6 a.m. I spent the next few hours trying to get some sleep in the cab of the truck, which was very cramped, but at least it was warm.

By 7 a.m. a few more trucks and horse trailers had arrived, but I was now getting worried that I would miss my connection from New York to Los Angeles. I had allowed twelve hours in New York to unload the horses, get across the airport to the passenger terminals and catch the plane. I had thought this would allow for delays and give me time for a wash and change. Travelling in close contact with horses and having to water and feed them would be a dirty job. It now looked as if our take-off might be delayed by twelve hours and I contemplated letting the O'Neills know that I might miss the flight, for by the time we arrived in New York it might be too late to stop John going the eighty miles to the airport to meet me.

But now things began to move and I was so busy helping to get the horses ready for loading that I did not have time to send a cable. Each horse had to be loaded into a narrow crate which holds three, side by side. The crates are then hoisted up to the level of the body of the aircraft, on a huge lift, then rolled into the plane and pushed into place on metal castors. They are then secured to the floor of the plane by heavy chains and are packed in as close together as possible. When it is fully loaded with thirty-three horses there is not much space left in a Boeing 707. There are a few seats at the tail end for the grooms, and to move along the aircraft one had to bend double, because the top of the crates meet the side of the aircraft about five feet up, owing to the curved shape of the plane. All the interior fittings had been removed and many of the windows blocked up to avoid breakage and I felt as if I was working in a tunnel.

The six horses in my charge were in the middle of the plane, and were two yearlings and four horses just out of training. One of them, being a highly-strung filly, had to be drugged to settle her down and I had to stand with her for the first two hours in case she tried to lie down. Although it seldom happens, great care has to be taken to prevent horses going down in the narrow stalls. If they do go down there is no way of getting them up and they would usually have to be destroyed to prevent them smashing the crate in a panic.

We had a very smooth flight, and after my tranquillised filly settled down I had no problems. We gave them hay and water twice on the eight-hour flight and this was not easy because we had to crawl under the heads and necks of the first two animals to reach the third.

We landed in New York half an hour before my Los Angeles flight was due to take off. Luckily, the owners of my bunch of horses arrived early and I was able to hand over to them. A kind member of the plane's crew offered to drive me across the airport to the passenger buildings and I rushed into the departure lounge as they were making the last call for boarding my plane.

Because of the cold in London I had been wearing a heavy Aran-type sweater and now it was covered in horse hair and hay. I hate to think what the other passengers thought, for I've observed that people going long journeys by plane always seem to be so smartly dressed. I did try to tidy up on the flight, but it was impossible to do much in the tiny space of the aircraft toilet. I arrived in Los Angeles looking as though I had just finished mucking out a stable yard. John was amused when he met me but I think he had given up being surprised at the unusual things I do.

CHAPTER TWENTY-TWO

IT WAS dark that evening before we got out of the city, but next day we drove around the Blue Jay and Lake Arrowhead area with Bambi and the boys. It is a beautiful part of the country, situated in 6,000-foot-high mountains, mostly covered in tall pine trees, with two lakes in the valley. Even at that time of year the weather was pleasant, and we drove to the inland side of the mountains, where the country turns into desert which stretches as far as one can see. That afternoon we went to the city and out to Burbank, near Hollywood, where John had Missie stabled. As soon as she heard John talking in the huge barn which held over a hundred horses, Missie whinnied, and she showed obvious delight when we arrived at her box.

John took her out and ran her up for me while I checked her all over for the various points I would require in a brood mare. As I had hoped and I think expected, from that point of view she was almost perfect, with an exceptionally lovely head. He then worked her for a short time in the area near the stable while I filmed them, as I wanted some record of someone else working a horse without a bridle.

After this we returned Missie to her box and went to visit a friend of John's who owned two fine Quarter Horse stallions. One was the very well-known Harmon Zero, and the other his half-brother Alven Zero, known as Jug Head for some unknown reason. They were both powerful big horses and Harmon Zero had done very well in both racing and show-ring, while Jug Head had an excellent temperament and had been used in all types of show business performances.

John and I suddenly thought it would be a good idea to get Missie covered by one of these horses before she left for Scotland. The owner of the stallions agreed to this idea as he had always liked Missie, and offered me free service to either of his horses. However, it was mid-winter and Missie had other ideas and did not come into season, although she was teased to the horse every other day.

That evening John showed me a letter from another party wanting to buy Missie and offering a considerably higher price than I could pay. John already knew the limit I could give for the mare and I told him he should accept the other man's offer. However, John knew this man wanted her only for a short showing campaign and after he had finished would pass her on to the best buyer. In the end John insisted he would only sell her to me, and I was pleased to have her.

The next day we returned to Burbank and went riding with Missie, Juggy, and with a friend of John's on an old Arab which he had had for well over twenty years. This was the first time I had been able to ride with John since I had taken up riding without a bridle and I found it interesting comparing our different ways and discussing the experiences we had each had in this type of work. After I had ridden Missie on a bosal for a couple of hours John said he would be quite happy if I felt I wanted to try her without a bridle. I did so, and she responded well although we do not use exactly the same aids. John and I must communicate to the horse in a similar way, for previously two good riders had tried to ride Don without a bridle and it was hopeless. Within minutes she had got very excited and upset and returned to the stable fast. This must be because of this lack of communication; many people have ridden Don *with* a bridle and had no trouble.

During the next few days we made frantic plans to get Missie across the States in time to catch the charter flight which was due to leave New York in two weeks' time. Then, leaving John to sort out the problems of getting all the required blood tests done in half the usual time, I had to return home.

The flight Missie was due to come in on was due to arrive mid-afternoon on Monday 16th December. I planned to leave home on Saturday morning, to drive the five hundred miles to Gatwick, thus allowing for bad roads at that time of year. John had phoned to tell me that Missie had left Los Angeles as planned, giving her nine days to reach New York in time for the flight. This should have been ample time but, owing to severe blizzards in central America, the truck had to take a long way round, via Arizona, New Mexico and up the east coast. Then on Friday night the charter company phoned me to say the truck had broken down and would not catch the flight. I cancelled my plans to drive to London and expected to have to wait two or three weeks before another charter plane was due. Suddenly, at nearly midnight on the Saturday, the American agent phoned from New York to say my mare had just arrived and would be put on the plane. It was a case of "drop everything" and drive south early the next morning, Sunday.

I left at 5 a.m. and, with a short stop that night, made Gatwick an hour before the plane was due to land. It was dark before they began unloading and jets were taking off on the next runway about a hundred yards from where we were. Some of the thoroughbreds were getting very upset by the noise, but Missie walked calmly out of the crate stall, over the tarmac and into my truck as if she had lived on an airport all her life.

When picking up horses from a foreign country one must not unload them again until they reach the stable where they are going to spend the two weeks' quarantine period. I was taking Missie all the way back to Aberdeen and she had now been travelling continuously for ten days — she must have a rest first. I stopped at a friend's farm situated near to the airport and was able to make a comfortable loose box for her in the truck by taking all the partitions out. I gave her supper and a deep bed of straw and within an hour she was peacefully lying down in the truck, probably for the first time in a week. The next day we had an uneventful run home and Missie settled in to our stable much more easily than

Lady had done. This was perhaps because she had not lived so close to the O'Neill family as Lady had, but had been frequently in livery stables.

CHAPTER TWENTY-THREE

I GAVE Missie a couple of days' rest, only leading her out to stretch her legs. Having had past experience of Don's jealousy I kept Missie out of her sight. On the third day I rode Missie in a bosal in case she was upset by her strange surroundings. The following day I had her shod and did a long ride without a bridle and she went really well. She appeared to listen for my aids as if I had trained her myself, which gave me a pleasant feeling, but I found it surprising for I had only known her for a few days. She appeared to have transferred her affection to me and would whinny whenever she heard me talking to the men in the yard, even though she could not see me.

For the next few days I rode Missie while escorting my usual morning rides, both in the indoor school and on hacks. She behaved splendidly without a bridle; the only problem I had was asking her to strike off straight into a right lead canter. She would break into canter on the left lead and then two strides later give me a flying change onto the correct lead. I tried all my usual methods to get a correct strike-off and even put her back into the bosal, but the only way I could get it at that time was to put her over a small jump as I asked for the stride-off. Very soon after she arrived I started putting her over small jumps and she loved this. Within a couple of weeks she was jumping all types of obstacle, both natural and artificial, up to about three feet. All this work was done bridleless, and she showed the same use of her head and neck as Don did.

About a month after Missie arrived, the local Riding Club ran a novice cross-country run. This is a ride over a course of natural obstacles, mostly stone walls, and it is ridden as a group, at varying speeds according to the conditions. This particular ride was going to be about five miles and I felt Missie was ready for it. I had clipped her out completely, and she was much admired by many of the other riders who had previously been doubtful about my Quarter Horses.

It was a cold, windy day, but Missie behaved well and jumped perfectly. Then, half-way round the course, a horse in front of me refused a wall. As we were going fairly fast, I swung Missie to the side to jump another part of the wall, which must have been just outside the safe, marked area. Although it looked like a safe jump, there was in fact a large boulder on the landing side. Missie landed almost on top of it and went lame for a few strides, but then seemed to recover so we continued the ride.

However, by next morning she had stiffened up and was very lame on one hind leg. As there was no filling and she was putting her weight on the leg, I did not get the vet at first, thinking she had pulled a muscle. After three days and no improvement I got the vet, who examined her thoroughly but could not find any definite injury. He also thought it must be a strained muscle high up in her quarters, and gave her mild pain killers and ordered a month's rest. This was hard now that she was clipped out in mid-winter, but he did not want her galloping round the fields. I took her for walks on a halter with plenty of rugs on. She used to lie down in her box quite often and loved me to sit and play with her and scratch her tummy.

It was now February and I thought this rest period might be a good time to try to cover her, in case she was difficult to get in foal, being an eight-year-old maiden mare. Luckily, she and Buck got on very well and she was covered without problems.

Don was not doing hard work because of being in foal and Missie was off, and thus I now had time to do more regular work with Buck, including gentle schooling. He was an extremely intelligent, responsive young horse and I soon found that I had developed a close relationship with him. Because he was a stallion I had no intention of doing serious work without a bridle. However, I was sure he was a horse who would try to give me his best at almost anything I asked of him, and in later years I was to find this to be absolutely true.

A month after the injury Missie still showed no improvement. I had started riding her on our walks, to cover more distance, and though she did not appear to be in pain her stride was uneven. The vet admitted there was no more he could suggest, so I arranged to take Missie south to one of the animal research hospitals. There they have large X-ray machines that can examine any part of an animal's body. They were also experimenting with faradism, which is a means of locating injured muscles by electric shock treatment.

On the journey Missie appeared to be upset by travelling on her own and would whinny every time the truck stopped unless I talked to her from the cab. I am sure she realised that her security of the past three months was once again going to be shattered, and I hated the idea of leaving her in a strange stable again. For the first two days I stayed at the hospital because a highly-strung horse will stand much more quietly without being tranquillised for X-rays if in the company of someone he knows and trusts.

With all their equipment and very knowledgeable horse vets it did not take long to discover the problem, but the news was not good. When she landed on the boulder while on the cross-country run, she must have jerked her off-hind leg violently sideways and in doing so had torn the ligaments holding the pelvis in place. Torn ligaments will never heal, and the bone had remained slightly out of position. The vets were not very hopeful of a complete recovery, but said that if she was left as she was it would be very unlikely that she could foal successfully. The treatment recommended was rather drastic but they said it was usually successful. It required that they gave her a total anaesthetic and by using sheer force manipulate the bone back into place. Although the ligaments would not heal, once the bone was back in place there was a chance that the muscles could be developed with exercise, to take the place of the damaged ligaments.

However, I was worried about the long anaesthetic that was required. Two years previously I had lost a top class thoroughbred stallion by having him anaesthetised for a minor operation, and by this time I had become very involved with Missie, who was such an affectionate little horse. But I decided to let them go ahead, and I returned home leaving her there, for the treatment required a few weeks of special exercise, under drugs, after the operation.

The next ten days were a ghastly worry until I got the news that Missie had come through the operation all right. She had to remain at the hospital for another two weeks under treatment. During these two weeks I did not have much time to worry about her. Although it was now the middle of April, we had the worst blizzard of the year. Philip and I woke up at 4 a.m. with driving snow beating against the windows. We had just started lambing and this could be a disaster. We struggled into the thickest clothing we could find and into the Range Rover, but had to fight our way through drifting snow to get to the field where the sheep were. The sight of that field in the half-light of early dawn was like a horror film, with dying lambs scattered all over the snow-covered frozen ground. The wind was so strong we could hardly walk into it, and the snow made it almost impossible to see where we were going. However, we struggled up the field picking up and carrying the pathetic little bodies as we went, the distraught mothers following us. Lambs have an amazing ability to recover if you can get them thawed out while there is any life left in them. Having got all the sheep together, Philip and his stockman, who had also wakened with the storm, got out the tractors and trailers, and after a great struggle we got all the sheep and lambs loaded into them. We then did something we have never done before. We drove them two miles to our indoor riding school and kept them inside there for the next ten days. Being able to keep them under cover saved the lives of over a hundred lambs.

Many farmers in our area lost nearly all that year's crop of lambs and some of them lost dozens of young cattle. The storm was so sudden, the animals got buried and could not be rescued before they either froze or starved to death.

Plate 6.
Mrs. Shuna
Mardon on
Strathdon.

CHAPTER TWENTY-FOUR

AT LAST I got news that Missie was ready to come home. She was not yet sound and the vets expected it would take three to six months of careful exercise under drugs to make her develop the muscle enough to make the stride even. When I arrived at the hospital she was in an inside box and so could not see into the yard, but she recognised the sound of my truck and immediately began to whinny. I am sure it is this kind of demonstration of affection which is the reward for the time spent really getting close to your horse.

The next two months were a series of hopes and disappointments, and by the beginning of June Missie was still unsound. I had to accept the fact that she was unlikely to make it for the Championships. However, by the end of June she was much better and working without any drugs.

We had almost run out of time, but I started seriously to school her in all movements required in the Pleasure Horse Class. I took her to a couple of English shows, just for the experience, for she had not learnt all the different paces required in hunter classes. At the first show she was crowd shy and did not concentrate on her work, but there was a great improvement at the second one.

There was now only one chance to qualify Missie for the Western Horseman's Association Championship Show, and that was at the East of England Show, which is the most important show to hold Western classes. I took three other Quarter Horses with me because there was to be a parade of Quarter Horses as well as the Western classes. This was lucky for me because it gave Missie a chance to get used to the size of the arena before having to compete in it.

The day was hot, with a series of terrific thunder storms, but Missie appeared to have accepted this new activity happily. She went very well in both the Western Pleasure and the Stock Horse classes, although she was a little uncertain of herself in the individual displays. We ended up second in the Pleasure class and third in the Stock Horse class, and this was enough, for first and second place winners qualify for the National Championships. I was pleased with her performance — the entries were large and the winners very experienced horses.

This was also Buck's first Show and he did well too, being ridden by Henry Depford; he was placed fourth and fifth in the respective classes. He and Missie were very much admired and Missie attracted a great deal of attention for the breed. I had done a short display in each parade, working without a bridle.

Shortly after this Show I had the chance to enter Missie again before the Championships. This time it was a smaller event and Missie went beautifully to win the Pleasure Horse class. One of my students, who had started riding only eighteen months earlier, came second on another Quarter Horse.

Over the next few weeks I worked Missie hard on all the show movements, and we only had arguments on flying changes. All this time I kept my fingers crossed for her soundness, until we came at last to the week of the Championships.

A friend and I set off south with a full truck, as I was taking Buck for Henry to ride, and a mare and foal were being returned to their owner after visiting our stud. We stabled the horses near the showfield and they settled down well after a long journey. This year the Show was being held in Northamptonshire.

The Show day was fine and Missie was on top form, and even Buck was much more settled than he had been at the East of England Show. There was a big entry for the Pleasure Horse Championship and Missie went really well, showing her smooth stride at all paces, while performing calmly and obediently. After the preliminary judging she was pulled in third, below two good Arabian horses. Then we were asked to do an individual display, including extended lope and figures of eight at the canter. Missie gave an almost perfect display and pulled us up into first place, as the other two were not as steady or accurate in their movements. This was a great thrill for me, for out of all the times I had competed in this event, this little horse had had the least preparation.

When we came out of the ring Missie, being a typical Quarter Horse, decided we had finished and went to sleep. The Press photographers wanted her picture, but nothing would make her stand up and look alert. In the Novice Pleasure Championship Buck went well and came second to an Anglo-Arab which was also a Grand Prix dressage horse.

Missie was in good form all day and won the Stock Horse class and the Pairs Pleasure Horse class, and would probably also have won the Trail class, for she negotiated all the obstacles perfectly but I took the wrong course. The final result was that she ended up as the High Point Champion of the day and the 1975 British Western Pleasure Horse Champion. This was a wonderful ending to many months of anxiety.

CHAPTER TWENTY-FIVE

ALL through the summer of 1975 Don had spent most of her
time out at grass and she did not appear to enjoy her enforced
holiday. I did ride her when escorting the slower riders, but
this was only once or twice a week. Towards the middle of
July she got very heavy and bad tempered towards other
horses.

On the evening of 23rd July Don was not very keen to be
caught and her udder was really hard, so I went to check her
in her loose box after supper. Although I knew she would not
worry about my presence I watched her very quietly so that
she was not aware of me and would act naturally. Whilst still
nibbling her hay she kept walking round her box and digging
her bed into a pile. These signs told me she was thinking
about foaling, and, knowing that two of my students were
longing to see a foal born, I went down and told them. I was
sure Don would probably like me to be around, but most
mares do not like an audience at foaling time. The girls
remained in a next door box from where they could watch
her through a window but could not be seen by her.

Don did not keep us waiting long and after lying down
and getting up a few times she started the actual foaling.
She had some difficulty when it came to the foal's shoulders,
as one of the forelegs was a long way in front of the other
and the elbow was causing an obstruction. After she had got
up and down again without helping the situation, I got a clean
towel and entered the box. As I had already been talking to
her, she was unworried and allowed me to wrap the towel

round the legs to give me a better grip and ease the backward one out level with the other. Within a few minutes she gave two more heaves and the foal was clear. Having made sure that his nose and mouth were clear of the afterbirth, I left her in peace to let nature take its course. After half an hour I came back and she was up and looking rather horrified as her little wet colt flopped about the box in his efforts to get up. Don had made a good job of drying him and it was a warm evening so I left them for another couple of hours.

As Don is half Arab and they are often rather silly mothers, I wanted to make sure she allowed the foal to suck before I left them for the rest of the night. When I came back at midnight the foal was up on his very long, wobbly legs and was searching all round his mother, trying to find the milk bar. He had the right idea, but Don did not know what she should do and was backing away from him. After I had held her still for about ten minutes the little colt found the udder and got hold of the teat. At first Don found his sucking ticklish, but after a few minutes she relaxed and he had a good feed before flopping back onto the straw.

The girls were delighted. This was the first foal they had seen being born although they had been working with me all through the stud season.

Next day was warm and sunny and Don was able to show off her new baby out in the field. When the vet came to give him the usual injections against tetanus and joint-ill, he said he would not have believed it possible a year ago.

Although Don was a very proud mother she still had complete trust in me and the early handling of her colt was made easy. We called him Donside Monarch, or Mickey for short. He was a very pretty foal, small and very fine of bone. Shortly after this, Don had the honour of having her photograph on the front cover of *Horse and Hound*. It had been taken while she was jumping a cross-country course without a bridle the year before.

CHAPTER TWENTY-SIX

ALL through this summer I had been working Buck lightly and, now that Don was busy with her foal and Missie was having her work cut down, I had much more time to devote to him. As mentioned before, he was an extremely intelligent, sensitive young horse and, although he could be a typically cheeky young stallion, he learnt quickly.

I had no intention of ever seriously working him, as a stallion, without a bridle, in case he was ever challenged by another horse. However, this did not prevent me building up a strong relationship with him, and this led to an unusual experience. One afternoon I had been repairing a fence round his field and he was grazing about a hundred yards away with his mares. As I came to the end of the job I realised that I was communicating with Buck although I had not talked to him aloud at all. It was a strange sensation, and I stood against the gate watching him. He had raised his head and was looking at me, then he walked once round his band of mares, left them, and came over to the gate. This was not unusual and I slipped a halter on and rode him down to the stable. I was so sure we were in mental communication I decided to put it to the test for my own satisfaction. I told the girls I was going to ride Buck without a bridle, and they both said that surely this was not possible as I had never taught him the independent leg aids. I saddled him up in an English saddle, with just a strap round his neck. I took him along the road to my jumping paddock, where I knew I had built a course of jumps he had not seen before. I worked him on the flat, circling and

turning at all paces, halting and reining back, with absolute
calm acceptance of all my commands. He is normally a rather
impetuous jumper, but this time I cantered him calmly round
a course of eight fences with no problems at all. As I relaxed
and was returning to the gate I remembered that he had
jumped the last two fences by coming in too close, and I
decided to do those two again. Then, before I gave him any
direct aid, I felt he knew exactly what I was thinking and he
considered he had done enough. He made no objection when
I asked him to turn back towards the jumping area, but when
I asked him to jump the last fence again, he stopped twice! I
smacked him firmly across the ribs and he jumped it well and
went home with no problems. Over the next few months I
worked Buck frequently without a bridle and found we
certainly had a close mental relationship. Unlike the two
mares, his attention was divided between me and his mares
and I would not have wanted to change this, for he was firstly
a very valuable stud horse.

With Buck I had a pure Quarter Horse with which I could
start serious competitive work to prove that the Quarter
Horse can compete successfully against more conventional
English horses. There are no Western shows during the winter
and I concentrated on getting his dressage and jumping work
up to competitive standard.

The first event I took him to was a Combined Training
event held in an indoor arena in Edinburgh. The arena was in
an old building and very spooky and full of pigeons which
lived in the rafters and on that particular day all the windows
rattled alarmingly in the high wind.

Buck had the ability to do very good dressage in the future.
This winter's events were only for practice, so I was not
surprised when he bucked and shied his way through the first
test with complete lack of concentration. The Quarter Horse
is known to accept new situations very quickly and by the
second test Buck had almost got over the spooks and went
well. In a Combined Training event the score of the dressage
is added to the points gained in the jumping section to give
the final results. This event was a novice competition, the

jumps being about three feet, and Buck gave me two clear rounds. This was good enough to give him a win with his second test and, as he was still only a three-year-old at his first event, many people were impressed. They were also amazed that he was a working stud horse and yet all through the day he stood around in a bunch of strange horses with no fuss at all.

This was just the start of a year in which Buck was to prove himself to be the most versatile four-year-old I had ever ridden. One of the main reasons I had gone into Quarter Horses was because of their wonderful temperament and ability to switch easily from one job to another. During the winter and spring I hunted Buck, show-jumped him, and won two more dressage tests on him, one of them taking place the day after he had been hunted. Then in the spring I got him really fit and rode him in a twenty-five mile competitive endurance ride, where he came sixth out of twenty-three entries.

After that he had a short rest before starting his stud work, but with his nature I was able to continue with his show work all through the stud season. He competed successfully in Working Hunter, Ridden Hunter and Inhand Hunter classes against thoroughbreds and on one occasion he won the Overall Hunter championship at an important show. He also continued his success in dressage and combined training events and switched easily back to Western work for the few Western shows.

Plate 7.
Strathdon, ready to
go into a Western
Trail Class.

CHAPTER TWENTY-SEVEN

JANUARY of 1976 was a cold, wild month, and I had Missie stabled every night in order to keep a close watch on her. The vets had warned me that her first foaling could be a very difficult one owing to her injury. Having ridden both the sire and the dam I felt certain that this foal could be a valuable one. I had intended to show Buck at a National Quarter Horse Show and Convention, which was being judged by a very experienced American. However, it was held over six hundred miles away, on 17th January, and Missie was due to foal on the 22nd. She had always been a very shy mare with strangers, hated vets, and did not trust the girls. I thought it more important to be on hand if she foaled early.

By this time she was very heavy and obviously uncomfortable, but otherwise fit and well. For about ten days I checked her three times each night and kept an infra-red lamp burning in the stable. On 28th January we had the wildest night of the winter. A terrific gale and driving snow, and the whole barn creaking and rattling with the wind, but Missie's box was warm and cosy with straw built up round all the walls.

For the past two nights her udder had waxed up, with no results, but that night she was very restless as well. When I checked her at 10 o'clock she whinnied as soon as she heard me in the barn, and again when she thought I was leaving. I collected some horse blankets and settled down to spend the night with her. By 11 p.m. she had started to foal and it was obviously going to be quite an effort, as she broke out in a sweat very soon after the first water had come.

However, there did not appear to be anything wrong, and she accepted a warm drink between contractions. She got very worried if I even left the box, so I collected everything I might need in one go. Then about 11.15 the foal's front feet appeared and much to my relief shortly afterwards I could feel its nose; because it was so slow I was afraid the head might have been turned back. Owing to the injury the pelvic girdle was extremely tight and therefore giving her a great effort to push the foal through it.

There was nothing I could do in the first stages, but once the front legs appeared I was able to help pull every time she strained. It was after midnight before the foal was clear, and about half-way through I thought it was dead because its tongue was blue. If a foaling takes too long the foal often dies, because the bloodstream from the dam is cut off by the pelvic pressure, and if the foal's ribs are still under pressure it cannot breathe and so dies from lack of oxygen.

Once it was clear I was able to rub it all over to get the circulation going, but for about ten minutes it hardly showed any sign of breathing, although I could feel its heart beating. Then suddenly it tried to lift its head and I guessed it would make it. Most mares break the cord by getting up and turning round to lick their foals, but Missie was exhausted and made no effort to get up.

It seemed that I would have to dry off the little one, but it is very important that a mare smells and licks her baby before it is cleaned, to be able to recognise it later. I carefully tied off the cord and then moved the foal round under Missie's nose and at first she looked horrified at it. However, the smell soon told her instincts what she should do and I left them and went to get clean warm towels. At this stage I was able to see that the foal was a bay filly — everything I had hoped for. I soon got the filly dry and lying under the lamp and then gave Missie a hot drink of gruel.

The wind was still howling through the roof of the barn, so I put a blanket over Missie to prevent her getting chilled and left them for an hour to rest. When I came back, Missie was up and madly licking her baby and trying to get her to stand up, by pulling and sucking her ears. After a short time of this she had sucked all the hair off the ears because the skin was so soft. I tied Missie up with a hot feed while I helped the filly onto her feet.

I ran into one more problem when the foal tried to suck, for Missie's udder was very hard and apparently tender, Every time the foal managed to find and tried to get hold of the teat Missie let out a wild squeal and jumped away. It took thirty minutes of holding her with one foot up before the foal got her first drink, but she was too weak to hold the teat. Eventually I milked Missie into a bottle and fed the foal by hand. I repeated this twice before morning and then the foal tried again herself and succeeded, although Missie still squealed whenever the foal butted her with her nose.

The first day the blizzard kept up all day and I just walked Missie round inside the barn for some exercise. On the second day the weather cleared and they were both able to go out in the field for about an hour. Even after her difficult birth, foaly was able to jump and gallop round Missie and we decided to call her Waccabuc Santana, which is the Red Indian name for Wind.

This little foal lived up to all my expectations for her, and turned into a real beauty, winning the only pure Quarter Horse class she was entered in that year. One day I hope she may follow her mother's successes under saddle, and she is certainly one horse I am sure I shall ride without a bridle.

After Don's foal was weaned, she had one other great honour. Don and I were asked to give a short diaplay of dressage and jumping without a bridle, for H.R.H. Princess Anne. The Princess came and had a chat with us afterwards but I would have liked to have had a much longer talk with her as she is such a talented horsewoman.

I still work Don almost entirely bridleless and expect to compete on her for many more years to come, as well as enjoying our hunting and hacking round our lovely country-side.

EPILOGUE, 1985

STRATHDON

Although I did not do much more competition work with Don after her first foal, I did do many more demonstrations all over the Country.

She is still with us now, and thoroughly enjoys hacking and light school work, when I have time. In 1981 she produced a second colt foal, this time by Buck, and we called him Waccabuc Stepper, in memory of John O'Neill's first bridle-less horse.

Don's first foal sadly had to be put down as a five-year-old, with a back injury, but I have just backed Stepper, and feel that he is going to be quite a character. I do not think we will breed Don again, because, although these "character" horses are great fun for the one person to whom they get attached, they are very difficult to sell, because they will never become the ordinary riding horse who will go well for anyone.

WACCABUC

Buck turned out to be everything I had ever hoped for in one horse. He was Western National High Point Champion four years running, and Quarter Horse National Versatility Champion for five years.

He is a very successful show-jumper and is now a Medium Dressage horse, which is as high as one can go in Scotland.

He does well in one-day events, endurance rides and working hunter classes, as well as being a super hunter.

In 1982 he was Reserve Overall Champion Quarter Horse of Europe, after a very exciting trip to the European Western and Quarter Horse Championship Show at Aachen, West Germany.

In ten years at stud, he has sired two Female Champions of Britain and one Grand Champion Stallion, plus many very successful jumpers and event horses from his part-bred offspring. He will always be our premier stallion and, at £200, one of the best bargains I will ever buy.

MISS BAY CHARGER

Missie sadly died after a mysterious injury in the field in 1980, at the age of only fourteen. However, she had produced five really super foals, including three fillies by Buck, the last one of which I kept and am now riding very successfully. The other two were colts by a young stallion I had imported in 1977.

One of these, Zero Depth Charge, turned out to be the best conformation stallion in Britain. He is nearly 16 hands high and has already been Grand Champion stallion of Britain twice, as well as regularly winning in open hunter classes. He also does very good dressage and was Western High Point winner in 1983, as a five-year-old.

He will never replace Don and Buck in my affections, but he is a superb horse.

FAMILY

My sons are now teenagers, and Sean is a very keen horseman but Keith still prefers engines, in the form of motor bikes at present. My sister, now Lorna Clarke, is still riding very successfully in 3-day events, and my Mother is still supporting both our horse activities in all kinds of ways.

STACY CASH

Stacy Cash, the first Quarter Horse I ever owned, hit the
headlines in 1985, when, at the age of 21 years, she produced
live twin foals. This is very unusual in horses, and the first
time in Quarter Horses in Britain. Both are golden dun colts,
and, although one was considerably larger than the other at
birth, they were both strong, healthy foals. In 13 years with
us, Stacy has given us 11 foals, and may not be finished yet.

I hope to have many more years of training and competing
on the Quarter Horses, who are now becoming very popular
in this Country. But nothing will ever quite compare with the
wonderful feeling of total communication and trust I had
with Don over those eight years we travelled and competed
together.

A couple of years ago, a very well-known dressage rider
was teaching in Scotland, and particularly asked to see Don
work. It must have been years since I had last asked for more
advanced dressage movements from her, but in minutes
she was going round the arena doing half-pass, shoulder-in,
counter-canter, etc., with a perfect bend and outline, as far
as her now rather portly figure would allow. Her visitor said
that if he had not seen it himself, he would never have believed
it was possible without a bridle.

Whatever happens to my other horses, Don is with us till
the end of her life, which could be another 10 or 15 years, as
her mother lived to the age of 34.